GW00357754

MINDFUL PROJECT MANAGEMENT

Central to the issue of improving project performance is the application of deterministic, probabilistic processes, and techniques to reduce human error. To that end, we as project managers often endeavour to implement and follow a project management methodology in the belief that we can reduce the scope for emerging ambiguous requirements, ill-matched resource needs and availability, contractual and funding constraints, and other unwanted uncertainties. However, such 'self-evidently correct' processes are not without their limitations.

The management of uncertainty needs to be viewed not from a procedural, 'stand-alone' perspective but from a behavioural, people-driven perspective – that is, Mindfulness. Mindfulness is a project-wide human capability to anticipate key events from emerging trends, constantly adapt to change, and rapidly bounce back from adversity. Resilient project managers are forward-thinking and able to foresee relevant scenarios that are likely to occur and which may have damaging effects on performance. We strive to be prepared for the best but also for the worst, and learning is nurtured and encouraged. We believe that with purpose, whatever uncertainty hits us, and regardless of the damage caused, we can prevent a crisis from happening in the first place. When a crisis occurs, we can recover and bounce back from shocks, quickly restoring 'normal' management.

This book goes beyond commonly accepted standards in project management and looks past mere compliance to determinism and probabilistic approaches to managing uncertainty. Relying on the power of mindful thinking, it identifies an art to manage uncertainty.

ELMAR KUTSCH is Associate Professor in Risk Management, Cranfield School of Management. Previously, he held a variety of commercial and senior management positions within the Information Technology (IT) industry. As a passionate skydiver and former project manager, his interests, both privately and professionally, revolve around the management of risk and uncertainty.

MARK HALL is Senior Lecturer in Project and Operations Management and Director of the MBA Programme in Birmingham Business School at the University of Birmingham. Previously, he worked at the Universities of Bristol and Bath. Before becoming an academic, Mark worked in the UK and internationally for several years as a surveyor and project manager.

MINDFUL PROJECT MANAGEMENT

RESILIENT PERFORMANCE BEYOND THE RISK HORIZON

SECOND EDITION

Elmar Kutsch and Mark Hall

Routledge
Taylor & Francis Group

LONDON AND NEW YORK

Second edition published 2020
by Routledge
2 Park Square, Milton Park, Abingdon, Oxon, OX14 4RN

and by Routledge
52 Vanderbilt Avenue, New York, NY 10017

Routledge is an imprint of the Taylor & Francis Group, an informa business

First edition published by Gower Publishing Ltd 2015

British Library Cataloguing-in-Publication Data
A catalogue record for this book is available from the British Library

Library of Congress Cataloging-in-Publication Data
Names: Kutsch, Elmar, author.
Title: Mindful project management: resilient performance beyond the risk
horizon / Elmar Kutsch and Mark Hall.
Other titles: Project resilience
Description: Second edition. | Abingdon, Oxon; New York, NY:
Routledge, [2020] | Earlier edition published as: Project resilience: the art
of noticing, interpreting, preparing, containing and recovering. | Includes
bibliographical references and index. |
Identifiers: LCCN 2020002881 (print) | LCCN 2020002882 (ebook) |
ISBN 9780367200916 (hardback) | ISBN 9780367497484 (paperback) |
ISBN 9780429259579 (ebook)
Subjects: LCSH: Project management. | Risk management.
Classification: LCC HD69.P75 K875 2020 (print) | LCC HD69.P75 (ebook) |
DDC 658.4/04—dc23
LC record available at https://lccn.loc.gov/2020002881
LC ebook record available at https://lccn.loc.gov/2020002882

ISBN: 978-0-367-20091-6 (hbk)
ISBN: 978-0-429-25957-9 (ebk)

Typeset in Minion Pro
by Swales & Willis, Exeter, Devon, UK

MIX
Paper from
responsible sources
FSC   FSC™ C013985
www.fsc.org

Printed in the United Kingdom
by Henry Ling Limited

CONTENTS

FOREWORD

Project resilience is poorly understood but much needed. Best practice project execution planning (PEP) including scheduling, budgeting, and risk management can only take the project management team so far. To put it bluntly, stuff happens. PEP relies upon important assumptions about the future that may or may not materialise. Against the baseline of PEP, project resilience addresses the inherent uncertainty at the heart of project execution in terms of both the emergent uncertainties around the internally generated interactions between the various elements within the project and the external shocks that undermine PEP assumptions. These often manifest initially in weak, ambiguous signals that need to be read carefully in order to respond appropriately.

Project resilience is therefore about the capabilities of the project team to sense change in PEP assumptions that has both cognitive and stakeholder engagement dimensions; about the speed and direction of the communications within the team and with stakeholders; and about the slack resource required to craft responses as possible threats become real challenges. Project resilience is therefore about both the competencies of the members of the project team and the design of the project organisation to be mindful, responsive, and creative as they manage project execution. The concepts in this book are important and they have influenced our own executive education on leading complex engineering projects. I commend it to you.

Graham Winch

Professor of Project Management, and
Academic Director for Executive Education at
Alliance Manchester Business School,
University of Manchester

The challenge

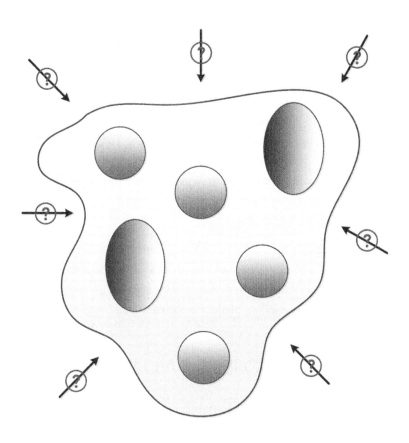

CONTENTS

We as project managers tend to treat projects with a strongly 'mechanistic' approach: the work can be broken down, executed and controlled as a series of interlocking parts. This is the technical, engineering-based conceptualisation, derived from the roots of the subject. While acknowledging the many benefits of this view, we take a different approach. We understand projects as 'organic' constructs, living and mindful entities existing for a finite period, consisting of people, supported by structures and processes. To continue the biological metaphor, this mindful organism is constantly challenged by environmental adversity. Success depends on remaining resilient, which we view as the ability to mindfully notice, interpret, prepare for, and to contain and recover from adversity.

This chapter is about those attacks on this entity we call a project. In this book, we will introduce you to ideas and mechanisms for resilience in project management and provide you with insights into how adversity can jeopardise project performance.

A LITANY OF PROJECT FAILURE

The media and literature are littered with examples of projects that have failed in terms of key parameters: time, budget and performance. They come from all sectors and all industries and can be found in the public and private sector. Complex projects with high levels of risk and uncertainty, such as military procurement, major construction, information technology and new product development projects are particularly vulnerable to failure.

For example, Berlin's Brandenburg Willy Brandt Airport (BER) is designed exactly like any other modern airport. It was expected to open in 2012, to replace the ageing airports of Tegel (in former West Berlin) and Schönefeld (in former East Berlin). In early 2019, though, this project showcase of German efficiency and engineering prowess was eerily deserted; no passengers had checked into this airport let alone taken off from it. Up to 90 km of cables were incorrectly laid, thousands of doors wrongly numbered, and the fire system was faulty.

The expected budget for this project amounted to roughly €2 billion. Six years later, though, it has been estimated to reach €7.5 billion, and the costs of maintaining an empty shell of an airport run into the millions of euros every year.

Meanwhile, in the United States, another project that hit the headlines refers to the municipal water supply project at Flint, MI. In early 2014, city officials decided to switch their city's water supply from the Detroit Water and Sewerage Department, who sourced their water from Lake Huron and the Detroit River, to the Karegnondi Water Authority, who pumped their water from the Flint River. The justification for such a switch should have resulted in savings in the range of $5 million.

To provide a safe supply of water to the inhabitants of Flint, corrosion inhibitors had to be added to the water treatment process. For reasons still under contention, this did not happen. The deteriorating water pipes started to corrode, causing the metals in the pipes to leach. Increased level of both iron and lead in the water were downplayed by city officials until it reached the airwaves of the national press.

In January 2016, both state and federal levels of government declared Flint an official disaster. As a short-term measure, the city switched back to sourcing their water from their original supplier, 18 months after the first switch. Significant damage to pipes requires an entire overhaul to the city's water supply system.

These are just two examples of major projects that have run into trouble and have failed to recover from such adversity. A common theme running through the many cases of failed projects is that, despite having applied a plethora of deterministic project management practices, they still do not deliver as expected, and the teams responsible for their delivery seem to lack the responsiveness to recover from failure. This is not because their approach to compliance by 'designing' adversity out of the project was inadequate. It is rather that the situation-specific novelty in each case is too much for the past-informed rules and procedures and that the organisations' ways of working do not accommodate the emerging reality of the situation.

This book looks at weaknesses with current thinking in project management and how project managers can develop a state of awareness and responsiveness – an art to be mindful – in the face of adversity. Our objective is to help project managers find ways to notice more, interpret adversity more realistically, prepare themselves better for it, and contain and recover from it quicker. In short, the book is about making projects and project managers more resilient through mindful project management.

THE EMERGENCE OF PROJECT MANAGEMENT

We need to start with a common understanding of what is meant by the term 'project'. A project is commonly defined as a temporary endeavour with a specific beginning and end. It is characterised by the achievement of unique goals and objectives, and resources are limited. In contrast to business-as-usual activities, which are repetitive and permanent, projects often involve greater uncertainty and complexity. At the outset of a project, managers may not know or understand exactly what they are required to achieve and how best to go about it, nor what changes and problems may be thrown at them. The discipline of project management has emerged in an attempt to aid managers facing these challenges.

A BRIEF HISTORY OF PROJECT MANAGEMENT

Mankind has achieved magnificent project outcomes for thousands of years. Marvels such as the Pyramids of Giza, the Great Wall of China, the Parthenon, and Stonehenge were constructed without modern-day techniques and software tools, although often with abundant yet expendable human resources. The twentieth century, though, experienced a new age of industrialisation and a drive towards repeatability of manufacturing outputs, mass-production and the pursuit of greater order and efficiency. Considered a milestone in the development of project management, Henry Gantt (1861–1919) developed the Gantt chart, which was quickly co-opted by managers to help control the project process.

The 1950s marked the emergence of the 'Program Evaluation and Review Technique' (PERT), deployed and exercised in the Polaris missile submarine programme. PERT displays how much time (involving the most likely, optimistic, and pessimistic estimates) is allocated to a component of a project, such as a project task. This enables projects to be analysed statistically. It lays down interdependencies between these components that allow the definition of a critical path; any deviation or change from that path will have an automatic influence on the end date of the project.

Such techniques are now commonly applied in planning modern projects and often represent the core technique of management by planning. However, it was not until the 1960s that the development of these techniques led to the recognition of project management as a discipline. In 1969 the Project Management Institute (PMI) was founded. This not-for-profit project management organisation is one of the most recognised member associations in the world. It advocates providing project managers with a universal set of tools and techniques to manage projects successfully.

As a consequence, the Project Management Body of Knowledge (PMBOK) Guide was published in 1987. Over the years, further internationally recognised frameworks and sourcebooks in project management have been developed, such as PRINCE2 and the

Association for Project Management's (APM) Body of Knowledge. They form part of a wider narrative advocating a set of normative procedures that, if applied correctly, are claimed to lead to success.

PROJECT SUCCESS AND FAILURE

Project success is a tricky concept. Projects are often assessed on the classic 'iron triangle' objectives of time, cost, and quality. Was it delivered on time, on budget, and did it meet the original performance specifications? If we rely on these three measures, then it may not be surprising if failure can be perceived as commonplace, but there are problems with this for several reasons. Criteria drawn up in the early stages may turn out not to be correct. Knowledge-generation is inherent in many projects, and initial expectations of accurate schedules and financial plans may be unrealistic. We need to be sensible about what we expect to find out as part of the work and adjust expectations accordingly. We do not argue with the importance of time, cost, and quality, but they do represent a rather limited, short-term perspective of what constitutes success – and failure – in projects. Longer-term user or customer satisfaction after a project has been implemented, or the development of new organisational capabilities, are not necessarily captured by these measures. Projects that meet specifications, are on time and budget may be considered a success, but if their outputs remain mostly unused because the end-users were not adequately consulted, then the investment was a poor one. Spending a little more time and money mid-way through to deliver what is necessary makes more sense, but if the organisational control and reward systems penalise this, they will drive the 'wrong' behaviours. Success and failure are thus far from clear-cut, and 'simple' evaluations are often misguided.

In the light of this wider perspective on the nature of success, many projects that could be regarded as failures might end up being resounding successes (and, indeed, vice versa). Many projects, though, are still scrutinised on their efficiency targets, often with limited regard to whether the outcome produced is as useful as was intended. This myopic view of projects does not come as a surprise given that, for example, long-term satisfaction scores include soft factors that are difficult to establish and measure.

We also have to realise that success and failure is a matter of perception. Perceptions matter and they vary. Different stakeholders can have quite different views of how well the work went, and a single consensus view can be rare. A user who receives exactly the system he or she needs may not be overly worried about the budget over-run, but this may be the primary concern of the finance manager. So, whose success are we measuring and when?

THE CHALLENGE OF UNCERTAINTY AND COMPLEXITY

A project's performance is constantly jeopardised by two components of environmental adversity: uncertainty and complexity. Project managers are often explorers in the dark, trying to establish a planned state in an environment that tends to generate adversity that is sometimes overt but sometimes only apparent when we stumble across it.

UNCERTAINTY

The concept of uncertainty is not an unidentifiable 'thing'. For example, when throwing an unloaded dice, it is possible to calculate exactly the probability of achieving certain results. This is what is known as aleatoric uncertainty, or true variability (from *alea* – the Latin word for dice): uncertainty reflects the unpredictability inherent to a stochastic process.

However, in many situations, we lack sufficient information to make a probabilistic assessment of something happening. If our dice were to constantly change its shape, it would be close to impossible to calculate the likelihood of future adversity. This particular type of uncertainty is known as epistemic uncertainty (*episteme* – from the Greek word for knowledge). In this case, our lack of knowledge about relevant variables leads to uncertainty, promoting an evaluative mode of thought of mindfully gauging the quality of what we think we know and do not know.

In more detail, Table 1.1 summarises some key characteristics of epistemic and aleatory uncertainty:

Table 1.1 *Distinguishing aleatoric from epistemic uncertainty (Fox and Ülkümen 2011, 22)*

	Aleatory	*Epistemic*
Representation	**Class of possible outcomes** Is represented in relation to a class of possible outcomes	**Single case** Is represented in terms of a single case
Focus of predictions	**Event propensity** Is focussed on assessing an event's propensity	**Binary truth value** Is focussed on the extent to which an event is or will be true or false
Probability interpretation	**Relative frequency** Is naturally measured by relative frequency	**Confidence** Is naturally measured by confidence in one's knowledge or model of the casual system determining the outcome
Attribution of uncertainty	**Stochastic behaviour**	**Inadequate knowledge**
Information search	**Relative frequencies**	**Patterns, causes, facts**
Linguistic marker	**'Chance', 'probability'**	**'Sure', 'confident'**

We may be uncertain about key aspects of the project. First, with goal uncertainty there may be a lack of clarity with regards to the goal to be achieved and the best way to get there. Imagine you start a project of a type you have not engaged in before. Neither you nor your stakeholders can fully define the goal of the project with confidence. This is not uncommon – many projects involve only vaguely definable outcomes that even key owners or sponsors struggle to specify. In R&D projects, for example, managers are faced with the challenge of specifying requirements, functions and outcomes, yet the reality is that knowledge will emerge as the work progresses.

The second dimension, approach uncertainty, relates to how the already unclear goal will be achieved. Not only is the precise goal uncertain, but so too is the path towards it. Imagine you know what the goal is that needs to be achieved, but you do not know how to get there. Although 'ways of working' in projects are often advocated by professional organisations such as the PMI as being universal, many projects have unique (and constraining) elements, such as the new technology involved or the relationships between the key participants. One size does not always fit all. The 'how' in the project can be a winding and uncertain path and, as such, project managers may have to alter their initially-planned approach.

Dynamic uncertainty encapsulates the condition of constant change. It is less a question of 'where to' (Goal uncertainty), or 'how' (Approach uncertainty), but one of 'what': what to do given continuous change in the environment.

Finally, a category of uncertainty that is often largely ignored by major project management frameworks is relational uncertainty. Uncertainty is ultimately in the eye of the beholder. Despite the plethora of project data, people need to make sense of what they see. The same data can lead to multiple interpretations, and hence, a variety of actions, which may be unhelpful. The sum of the responses to differing perceptions may add to the level of ambiguity and confusion.

Reflection *How well do the following statements characterise your project? For each item, select one box only that best reflects your conclusion.*

Goal uncertainty	Not at all		To some extent		To a great extent
The outcome of the project is wide open.	1	2	3	4	5
We cannot quantify or qualify the goal with confidence.	1	2	3	4	5
There is nothing like this out there.	1	2	3	4	5

Approach uncertainty	Not at all		To some extent		To a great extent
Our ways of working do not apply to this project.	1	2	3	4	5
We have never done anything like it.	1	2	3	4	5
We need to take one step at a time.	1	2	3	4	5

Dynamic uncertainty	Not at all		To some extent		To a great extent
Nothing remains the same here.	1	2	3	4	5
It is like standing on quicksand.	1	2	3	4	5
Many changes are going on at once.	1	2	3	4	5

Relational uncertainty	Not at all		To some extent		To a great extent
No one is on the same page.	1	2	3	4	5
We all have a different understanding of where to go and how to do it.	1	2	3	4	5
Perceptions of uncertainty vary.	1	2	3	4	5

Scoring: Add the numbers. If you score higher than 9 in each category, please define which aspects are uncertain. If you score 9 or lower in a category, it might be worth checking that your colleagues agree. A 'Not at all' answer may indicate that you are underestimating the extent of uncertainty.

COMPLEXITY

The previous assessment unpacks the extent to which you perceive your project to be uncertain. Be aware that not only risk (aleatoric uncertainty) and epistemic uncertainty may derail your project. There is also a second element of adversity: complexity.

In a tightly coupled project, characterised by 'time-dependent processes', 'little slack' and 'invariant sequences of operations' (Perrow 1999), incidents can occur from initial (potentially small) failures building on themselves and rapidly becoming larger, triggering a sudden crisis (see Figure 1.1).

In a loosely coupled project, on the other hand, risk and uncertainty have limited direct implications for the other components (e.g. tasks, resources) in a project. The project does not destabilise overnight, and this allows a longer incubation phase – a creeping crisis – in which one has the opportunity to carry out some forms of intervention.

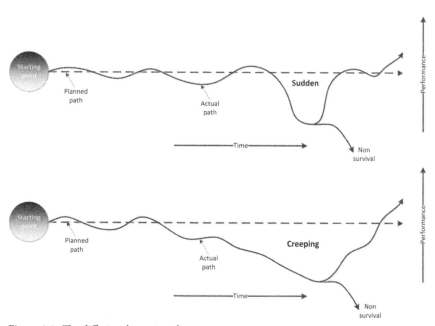

Figure 1.1 *The differing dynamics of crises*

Most projects do not face such a sudden collapse; they generally face a creeping erosion of performance, a 'death by a thousand cuts', a crisis that gradually builds. Projects tend to have a prolonged incubation phase, where adversity gradually builds to a crisis. However, in many cases, we as project managers mindlessly ignore those warning signals of an impending crisis. We tend to 'wake up' at a stage when a crisis or disaster can not be averted anymore.

Reflection — *How well do the following statements characterise your project? For each item, select one box only that best reflects your conclusion.*

Complexity	Not at all		To some extent		To a great extent
There is a lot of redundancy (e.g. time buffers) in our project.	1	2	3	4	5
Not every task has to go right the first time.	1	2	3	4	5
We have time to correct failures.	1	2	3	4	5
What is happening is directly observable.	1	2	3	4	5

Scoring: Add the numbers. If you score higher than 12, your project is relatively loosely coupled, with a lower chance of small failures rapidly triggering a crisis. If you score 12 or lower, please think whether the project needs to be 'decoupled', that is to say, whether complexity needs to be reduced to allow for timely interventions.

THE EVOLUTION OF RISK MANAGEMENT

The evolution of risk management – like many other planning mechanisms in project management – is characterised by the desire for certainty, quantification and the ability to prepare in advance for future events. In the distant past, people were guided by fate and faith in God's will. Indeed, the future was perceived to be at the mercy of the gods. These long-held fundamental beliefs started to be challenged during the Renaissance (fourteenth to seventeenth century), a period of turmoil, in which the shackles of superstition were challenged, and inquisitive people such as Pascal and Fermat embraced the concept of forecasting and of building the foundations for the theory of probability.

Probability theory evolved quickly into a method of organising, leading to, for example, the mathematical basis for the insurance industry. Until the early twentieth century, human imagination was driven by repeatability and statistical analysis of the past to inform the future, and many of our modern approaches are based on probabilistic forecasting and decision-making driven by a concept called Expected Utility Theory (EUT). EUT states that decisions about risks are made by comparing their expected utility values, for example, the weighted sum of probability multiplied by impact, so that the utility of decision-making choices is weighted according to their probabilities and outcomes. Consider the following simplified example shown in Figure 1.2.

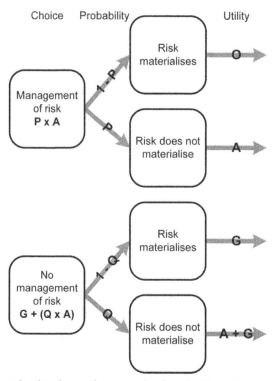

Figure 1.2 *Expected utility theory: the expected utility of taking risk response actions is* $((1 - P) \times 0) + (P \times A) = P \times A$. *The expected utility of not taking risk response actions is* $((1 - Q) \times G) + (Q \times (A + G)) = G + (Q \times A)$.

In the diagram, the probability of avoiding risks in a project through the execution of a risk response action is P, and without risk actions, Q, with P larger than Q and 1 – Q larger than 1 – P. The utility of avoiding risks (relative to the cost of materialised risk) is A, and the utility of no actions (relative to the cost of those actions) is G, while A is assumed to be greater than G. The decision by the project manager to take actions or not depends on the utility of avoiding the materialisation of uncertainty (benefit) while committing resources (cost), and on the relative magnitude of the objective or subjective probabilities.

EUT is a basic model of rational choice that underpins most methodologies for taking risky decisions and is generally regarded as a very useful and effective framework for decision-making under conditions of aleatoric uncertainty. However, the often 'blind' adherence to the principles of EUT and the resulting illusion of certainty was shattered by two bloody World Wars and, in more recent times, by major disasters such as the collapse of Lehman Brothers, the world recession, and the rise of world terrorism. Emerging criticism up to the present day has challenged the commonly adopted and advocated view that the past, if repeated often enough, can confidently inform the future:

> *Those who live by the numbers may find that the mathematically inspired techniques of modernism have sown the seeds of a destructive technology in which computers have become mere replacements for the snake dancers, the bloodlettings, the genuflections, and the visits to the oracles and witches that characterized risk management and decision making in days of yore.*
>
> (Bernstein 1996, 51)

WHAT DO WE MEAN BY RESILIENCE?

In its broadest sense, resilience can be seen as the capacity of a system to absorb disturbance and reorganise while undergoing change, so as to retain essentially the same function, structure, identity and feedbacks. This requires an understanding of what constitutes a system. A system is a set of elements that interact with each other and create emerging properties as a whole. Systems have functionality in that they exhibit behaviour. They also contain subsystems, which are groups of elements within the system that may, themselves, have similar properties. All systems interact with their environment as they exist within a given context, and have delineated boundaries. Systems interact with their environment to source inputs and produce outputs. Finally, they are purposeful in that they are identified by stakeholders to be of interest. So, when we talk of resilience, what we are talking about is the resilience of an entity that is, itself a system.

Resilience can be classified into several broad categories:

- Engineering (materials resilience);
- Ecology (resilience of the natural environment);
- Psychology (resilience of individuals);
- Sociology (organisational resilience).

It is the last of these that is of interest to us. This is not to say the others are not important (and may, indeed, impinge upon organisational resilience) but the focus of this book is on organisational resilience and, in particular, a specific form of organisation – the project as a mindful system, a 'living' organism.

The root concept of resilience can be seen in early ecological studies and is epitomised by the Panarchy model (Gunderson and Holling 2001). This model is often seen as a figure-of-eight diagram, always looping around in the process of continual change and renewal. It has four distinct but inter-related phases or stages.

1. Growth phase. This is where new opportunities and available resources are exploited and normally comes with weak interconnections and weak regulations. Pioneers and opportunists are frequently successful in this phase. Systems may experience numerous growth phases, and each one may or may not resemble previous growth phases.
2. Conservation phase. In this second phase, energy and capabilities are stored, and material accumulates. This stage is characterised by developing, increasing and stronger connections and

regulations. More conservative but also more efficient specialists take over, and the system becomes increasingly stable and rigid. However, with this stability comes a commensurate loss of flexibility. There is an increasing dependence on existing structures and processes in this phase and, as a result, the system is increasingly vulnerable to disturbance.

3. Release phase. In this third phase, a shock to the system means it 'comes undone'. Resources are released, and all kinds of capital (social, natural, economic) leak away. Connections break and regulation weakens. This phase is characterised by chaotic dynamics, uncertainty and destruction.

4. Reorganisation phase. Finally, the destruction shows creative potential and options emerge. Previously suppressed pioneers or invaders show up, and the future is 'up for grabs'. In a perpetuating system, there is a process of restoring. However, this restoration is characterised by novelty, invention, and experimentation. Released capital can regroup around new opportunities. This phase may (or may not) end with a new identity.

A crucial component of this model is that after the shock of the release phase, there may be no reorganisation phase if that shock is so severe that it destroys the system. The metaphor often used (and where the Panarchy model was developed) is one of a forest. It grows from saplings and small plants in the growth phase. The pioneers are the many different species vying with one another. Ultimately, some dominant species gain dominance and the forest will enter a conservation phase, where it grows and becomes stable. Imagine there is a sudden forest fire (a shock to the system) that destroys many of the trees and other plants of the forest. It is now well-understood in ecology that forest fires are crucial to the continued growth, new development, and subtle change of forests. After a forest fire, the forest will go into a reorganisation phase and, eventually, enter the growth phase and the cycle begins once again, in perpetuity. However, imagine the shock to the system is that bulldozers destroy the forest, strip away all the trees and the land is turned into monoculture farmland or grazing land. The forest is no more, and there is no reorganisation phase leading to a new growth phase.

This model can apply to organisations (or people, or materials) as much as it can to ecological systems. More precisely, organisational resilience can be defined as '*the maintenance of positive adjustment under challenging conditions such that the organisation emerges from those conditions strengthened and more resourceful*' (Vogus and Sutcliffe 2007, 3418). In this sense, organisational resilience is not about responding to a one-time crisis or about rebounding from a setback (the oft-stated 'bouncebackability') but is rather about continuously anticipating and adjusting to deep, secular trends that can permanently impair the earning power of a core business and about having the capacity to change before the case for change becomes desperately obvious.

Organisational resilience, as a concept, raises two issues for organisations. First, it is difficult for organisations to get good at something (resilience) at which you do not have much practice. Shocks to organisational systems might be frequent or infrequent, but organisational-threatening shocks do not come very often, and so organisations (for many of the reasons we address in this book) do not practise at getting good at being resilient. Second, there is the question of whether people in organisations are more concerned with mere survival in a world of uncertainty or whether they seek to thrive.

There are also three major issues that scholars, commentators and practitioners face when they think about resilience, none of which is easily resolved. Is resilience context-specific? Some organisations seem to be resilient in some circumstances but not others, so how can this be explained? There is also no obvious way to measure resilience as for many people, it is a vague, fuzzy thing that's hard to understand. This means that there is no obvious way of generalising to organisations everywhere. Finally, how is resilience to be judged? You cannot just wait for a disaster to happen to find out whether organisations are resilient, and looking at organisational inputs is not always the answer as some organisations that do not plan actually perform very well during a crisis. For example, some smaller organisations tend to do very little planning and, despite this, can do very well in times of crisis.

Despite these problems, issues and challenges with the concept of organisational resilience for scholars and practitioners alike, there is no doubt that resilience as a concept has captured the imagination of business leaders worldwide, looking for an answer to the levels of uncertainty and complexity we all face.

WHAT THIS BOOK IS ABOUT

This book has two purposes. First, it offers a glimpse into our tendencies to be mindless in the face of uncertainty and complexity. It endeavours to challenge the often held view that quantification of the future, informed by the past, and the 'automation' of actions can be an appropriate substitute for flawed human cognition.

The second purpose of this book is driven by the need to look beyond the risk horizon. In the short term, our risk horizon is far more measurable and tangible (see Figure 1.3). The past allows us to make some judgement about the near future. In this respect, commonly accepted standards in project management may serve us well to address aleatoric uncertainty; usually, such effort to address aleatoric adversity, in advance of it happening, is satisfied through the key discipline of probabilistic risk management.

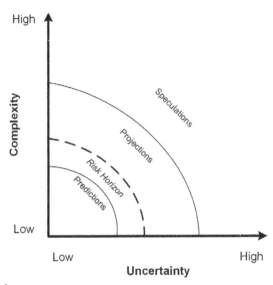

Figure 1.3 *Risk horizon*

The further out we move beyond the risk horizon, though, the greater the amount of epistemic uncertainty. We face diminishing precision, and situations are more open to interpretation. Traditional project management tools and techniques are limited in helping us with epistemic uncertainty. Instead of predominantly relying on hindsight as a predictor for the future, we need mindful approaches to deal with projections and speculations so that we are not caught out by the complexities in a project.

We will provide insights into the art of mindful project management that leads to a state of resilience beyond the risk horizon. This requires us to notice epistemic uncertainty more successfully, to be able to interpret uncertain situations more effectively, to prepare ourselves and our projects adequately for epistemically uncertain situations and, importantly, to recover swiftly from issues after they occur.

But beware! It is not a book that should be used as a manual or set of standard operating procedures. It is neither comprehensive nor do we claim to have discovered the 'Holy Grail' of mindful project management. The book's purpose is to guide, not to prescribe. It is best used as a trigger for a thinking process to define your own unique approach to managing epistemic uncertainty. Ultimately, it has been written to challenge conventional wisdom in project management and to address the rationale for mindful practices.

This book consists of eight chapters, each based on a separate stage of managing epistemic uncertainty through mindfulness. This chapter sets the scene. Chapter 2 aims to distinguish between two archetypes of project management by exploring one of the most puzzling defeats in modern military history. Chapter 3 is about the art of noticing, how to anticipate the immeasurable and the unpredictable. In Chapter 4, we look at the question of how to make sense of epistemic uncertainty and how to judge it. A nuanced appreciation of an uncertain environment is followed by guidance for project preparation and readiness for it in Chapter 5. Containing epistemic uncertainty, responding appropriately, and receiving support in doing so is at the forefront of Chapter 6. Chapter 7 acknowledges that not all adversity can be designed out of a project. It is not a question of 'if' but of 'when' a crisis strikes and how we can recover from it. Chapter 8 brings it all together, and there we reflect on how to activate and maintain a permanent state of project resilience through mindful project management. Chapter 8 provides you with a simple toolkit to start the process of being mindful in project management.

Chapters 3 to 7 proceed in a specific format. Each has four main sections, tackling the 'lures' that make it difficult for a project manager to be mindful, the role of leadership in driving mindful approaches in projects, and, finally, the way relationships across projects teams can be managed to ensure resilience is established and maintained beyond project boundaries. Each chapter is concluded with a vignette, a brief evocative description of a historical case study, as well as a self-assessment.

A SECTION ON LURES

The human brain is an amazing and incredibly powerful machine of synapses and neurons. But the brain is also fallible. It is not a super-computer but has evolved as a social machine. The information it receives is partial and localised (what we sometimes call culture). As a result, our behaviour is subject to cognitive biases, those annoying glitches in our thinking that cause us to make questionable decisions and reach erroneous conclusions. We are intuitive, emotional, and partial beings – we are human. It is important to distinguish between cognitive biases and logical fallacies. A logical fallacy is an error in logical argumentation (e.g. ad hominem attacks, slippery slopes, circular arguments, appeal to force, etc.). A cognitive bias, on the other hand, is a genuine deficiency or limitation in our thinking – a flaw in judgement that arises from errors of memory, social attribution, and miscalculations (such as statistical errors or a false sense of probability).

As a result, we frequently behave mindlessly in the way we deal with uncertainty, in the way we perceive it, in the way we understand it and in the way we respond to it. We will start each chapter with some of these behavioural 'shortcomings'. People can walk, to some extent, 'brainlessly' through projects, driven by the original plan and what they are told to do. All we are doing in this section of each chapter is to point out some of the behaviours, learnt and emotional, that make the management of adversity difficult. What we ask is that project managers understand that these fallibilities exist; we hope you see our suggestions as ways of helping to overcome fallible human cognition.

A SECTION ON ENABLERS

To deal with our fallibilities and our propensity to follow routines and procedures in a mindless fashion, we would like to suggest examples of 'good practice' – what a project manager could do (with an emphasis on 'could'). We want to emphasise that anything we suggest that could be done to manage epistemic uncertainty is context-specific. What works in one context may not work in another. These are not hard-and-fast rules.

A SECTION ON LEADERSHIP

Having suggested the 'what' (although intentionally non-prescriptively), we follow with the 'how' of implementation. If one leadership style has seemingly conquered the project management world, it is that of transactional leadership. Transactional leadership relies very much on compliance with process and procedures in which, as much as possible, situated human cognition is eliminated as a source of error through the imposition of rule-based behaviour. This approach does work if the project risks are predictable, measurable, and controllable, and people working on the project behave in reliable, rational ways. Unfortunately, management is rarely this straightforward. Mindful project managers, however, do not lead by replacing 'thinking'; they facilitate flexibility in mindsets and empower people to learn and apply situational and professional judgement. They foster information flow and provide a culture of support and encouragement.

A SECTION ON RELATIONSHIPS

Projects are social entities, often with a multitude of internal and external stakeholders. Whereas stakeholders add complexity, they can also be used as resources to manage epistemic uncertainty more effectively. Managing epistemic uncertainty can be a journey of painful ignorance (Kutsch and Hall 2010), sometimes on an enormous scale. Embracing the 'unknown' mindfully means managing and educating stakeholders. Reluctance to give in to temptation and consider the future as certain is only the beginning of stakeholder management. Not least, it is an emotional rollercoaster that requires some dedicated preparation and intervention.

All the chapters and sections in this book are complemented by two types of vignettes – indicated by text boxes – of best practices and evocative syntheses of key social and cognitive biases that challenge our ability to be collectively mindful:

TEXTBOXES ON SOCIAL AND COGNITIVE BIASES

There is an incredible amount of written work on social and cognitive biases that constrain our ability to be mindful to uncertainty. By default, we are biased to adopt a certain direction of decision making, often to the detriment of a collective mind. The book section on 'Lures' will provide you with a few mini-literature reviews on memory or cognitive biases; we review the current state of knowledge on some of the key biases that inhibit our ability to mindfully lead in a project environment.

TEXTBOXES ON MINDFUL PRACTICES

We try to learn from the best and try to understand what they do and why. While the discussions in this book draw on a wide range of research conducted both by the authors and others, we have selected three organisations which we believe have a track record of successful project delivery (with only the occasional hiccup) and, thus, epitomise some of the points we seek to make. They all carry out project work in a world of uncertainty and complexity, yet they prevail. They create a state of organisational and project awareness beyond the past and ready and prepare themselves for a future characterised by projections and speculations. When a crisis cannot be averted, response enactment is swift and pragmatic. Divergence from the expected plan does not result in simply tightening rules and procedures, but includes questioning project resilience in the widest sense possible.

MINDFUL PRACTICES

OUR CASE COMPANIES

The Technology Partnership Group (TTP Group) is a technology and product development company formed in 1987. They operate in several diverse technology areas including industrial and consumer products, microdevices, medical and life sciences technology, and electronics. Their core offering is the rapid development of challenging new technology, which is enabled through their depth of scientific, engineering and business capability. TTP is one of Europe's leading independent product development companies, serving clients worldwide. The founding group of 30 investor employees had all worked for PA Technology, part of the PA Consulting Group. TTP remains majority employee-owned. They are located close to Cambridge, with around 300 staff.

TTP is an operating company within the TTP Group. Other companies in the group include TTP Venture Managers, which manages an early-stage technology investment fund, TTP Labtech, which supplies instrumentation and custom automation to the Life Sciences sector, and Tonejet, which operates in the commercial and industrial printing markets. TTP Group also owns Melbourn Science Park, Cambridge UK, where TTP is based.

TTP operates in a highly uncertain business environment. Their core business is the creation of new technology, so there is always a degree of uncertainty in each of the 70–80 projects they might be working on at any given time. TTP has been involved in developing numerous technologies which then find applications in all sorts of areas. For example, TTP has been developing medical technologies such as the Bio-Seeq nucleic acid detection device. An example of a project that cut across organisational boundaries was the Sterishot, an obstetric surgical tool that combined engineering capabilities with human factor analysis to devise an ergonomic device to do the job. Another area in which TTP has undertaken development projects is in communications technology. Examples include the development of terrestrial and satellite digital technologies for devices like the Roberts solar-powered DAB radio and the development of the hardware for Vodafone's packet radio broadcast services.

Many of the technologies that TTP devises go on to be incorporated into products for mass or batch production and may be incorporated into devices that are used every day by companies and consumers.

The Aviva Group has a history stretching back more than three centuries. Over the years, many companies in several countries have been part of their rich history, including Norwich Union, General Accident, Delta Lloyd, and Hibernian. In 2000, the Group changed its name to Aviva, a palindrome chosen for its worldwide appeal and ease of pronunciation in many tongues.

With a history traceable back to 1696, the group prides itself on being the oldest mutual life insurer. Being one of the oldest fire insurers as well as the first and only insurance company to hold royal warrants are amongst its notable achievements.

Currently, Aviva provides 31 million customers with insurance, savings, and investment products. It uses project management skills and techniques to deliver major changes and specific project objectives to support its overall plans. The types of change typically handled as 'projects' are customer service enhancements and digital innovation. An example of each type is given below.

In 2014, as part of its commitment to improve its customer service, Aviva became the first UK insurer to publish its customer claim reviews online to give new customers more information about the service they can expect to receive and, also, to provide an open and public forum for customers to feedback about their claims experiences.

The service works by sending an email to customers after they have had a claim settled, asking them to write a review and give a rating for the service they have received. Customers can give a rating out of five and write a short review which may then be posted on the website, commenting on the service, how the claim has been processed and the overall experience. Both positive and critical reviews are posted online to give customers an overall view of the service as well as the overall rating.

Intel Corporation is an American organisation specialising in chip development and manufacturing. Back in 1968, two scientists, Robert Noyce and Gordon Moore, founded Intel – the portmanteau abbreviation for INTegrated ELectronics – with a vision to produce semiconductor memory products. By 1971, they had introduced the world's first microprocessor. Most widely known for processors, Intel is involved in the research and development of a variety of products and services related to communications and information systems. Its headquarters are located in Santa Clara, and by 2013 the company had over 107,000 employees worldwide.

An example of an activity Intel is engaged with is a high-value-adding project, destined to provide predictive analytics to Intel's sales organisation. This is to help the Intel sales force – Intel works with over 140,000 resellers who specify, design, build, and resell Intel-based technology products and solutions – optimise its account management and increase estimated incremental revenue.

In the beginning, Intel sold components to distribution, distribution sold to resellers and then resellers built the final product to be sold to end-users. The market trend toward smaller mobile devices has changed channel dynamics. Larger original design manufacturers (ODMs) and original equipment manufacturers (OEMs) are now building the end product, such as a laptop, business Ultrabook device, or tablet, and then selling that product to distributors, who in turn sell it to resellers. The sales organisation tracks Intel components that are sold to the ODMs and OEMs, but little data are available after that. The result is that the sales organisation does not have the data it needs to support the reseller; specifically, what exactly the reseller is marketing that includes Intel technology. With a diverse customer base, the sales organisation needed assistance prioritising which customers should receive the most support, determining the optimal time in the customer's buying cycle to contact them, and deciding what products or support to offer.

Intel IT has developed an advanced predictive analytics solution to identify and prioritise which resellers have the greatest potential for high-volume sales. The enterprise-level, end-to-end predictive analytics engine is directly responsible for a portion of the sales organisation's increase in estimated incremental revenue.

With this book, we hope to help you on a journey towards a state of mindful project management, with the purpose to increase and maintain project resilience, by elaborating the 'what', the 'how' and the 'why'. We offer a set of principles and a platform to reflect on your own context and your own projects, with self-assessment questionnaires at the end of each chapter. It is ultimately YOU, who decides what is best applied to managing adversity in the form of uncertainty and complexity, both efficiently and effectively.

REFERENCES

Bernstein, P. 1996. "The New Religion of Risk Management." *Harvard Business Review* 74(2): 47–51.

Fox, C. R., and G. Ülkümen. 2011. "Distinguishing Two Dimensions of Uncertainty." In: *Perspectives on Thinking, Judging, and Decision Making*, edited by W. Brun, G. Keren, G. Kirkebøen, and H. Montgomery, 21–35. Oslo: Universitetsforlaget AS.

Gunderson, L. H., and C. S. Holling. 2001. *Panarchy: Understanding Transformations in Human and Natural Systems*. Washington, DC: Island Press.

Kutsch, E., and M. Hall. 2010. "Deliberate Ignorance in Project Risk Management." *International Journal of Project Management* 28: 3.

Perrow, C. 1999. *Normal Accidents: Living with High-Risk Technologies*. Princeton, NJ: Princeton University Press.

Vogus, T. J., and K. M. Sutcliffe. 2007. "Organizational Resilience: Towards a Theory and Research Agenda." *Conference Proceedings – IEEE International Conference on Systems, Man and Cybernetics*, 3418–22.

CHAPTER TWO

Archetypes of project resilience

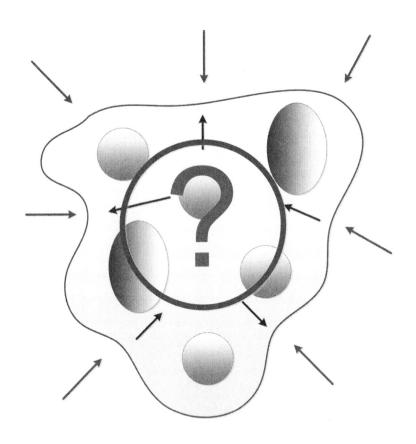

CONTENTS

In the previous chapter, we introduced the idea of projects as organic, complex entities. The resilience of a project organism is aided by the people inhabiting it being aware of their surroundings and potential disturbances. Ideally, the project resists, absorbs adversity and adapts to these disturbances without collapsing. In this chapter, we continue on the road to resilience by introducing and evaluating the archetypes of project resilience. One archetype is based on rules and procedures, stripping the organism of situated thinking, and relying wholly on predetermined responses to risk. The other allows human situated cognition – mindfulness – to flourish, to counter the impact of uncertainty. We use a case study in which these two fundamentally different styles of management 'clashed' with each other: the Fall of France in 1940. In it, we analyse how uncertainty was managed by the opposing parties, and what led to one of the most puzzling defeats in modern military history.

A 'PROJECT' WITHOUT PARALLELS

We could have chosen from a whole range of cases to provide a compelling insight into rule-based and mindfulness-based approaches to managing uncertainty in a project. The Fall of France in 1940 (Kutsch 2018) at the hands of Nazi Germany offers a compelling insight into the two archetypes of managing uncertainty, as these approaches stood in direct competition with each other in the most dramatic way possible.

'WE ARE BEATEN; WE HAVE LOST THE BATTLE'

On 15 May 1940, Winston Churchill, still in bed, was called by Paul Reynaud, the French Prime Minister:

> He spoke in English, and evidently under stress. 'We have been defeated.' As I did not immediately respond, he said again: 'We are beaten; we have lost the battle.' I said: Surely it can't have happened so soon? But he replied: 'The front is broken near Sedan; they are pouring through in great numbers with tanks and armoured cars.'
>
> (Jackson 2003, 9)

Only five days earlier, on 10 May, six German armies attacked the Low Countries (Holland, Belgium, Luxembourg) and crossed the river Meuse at Sedan and Dinant, two small French towns. The plan for the invasion of France, code-named Fall Gelb (Operation Yellow) was not the physical destruction of the French Army but, rather, the immediate collapse of their morale and, subsequently, the military defeat of France. The Oberkommando des Heeres (German High Command) was convinced that a long drawn-out war could not be won given the strength of the French Army and their Allies, and the logistical shortcomings on the German side. Hence, after a series of unconvincing operational plans bearing strong similarities to the Schlieffen plan used in 1914, and postponements of the offensive due to security leakages and weather, the Manstein plan (named after Lieutenant-General Erich von Manstein) was backed by Adolf Hitler and operationalised. The directive, produced on 24 February 1940, solved the long-disputed question of where the emphasis of the attack should be. In contrast to the original plan, it was not to be in the North with Army Group B, who might have bypassed the Maginot line (a mighty line of fortifications constructed along France's borders with Germany and Italy). Instead, Army Group B was allocated the role of a 'matador's cloak' to lure the bulk of the French forces into Belgium, away from the new centre of gravity, and into a trap where they would be encircled and destroyed.

In contrast to WWI, the weight of the armoured drive shifted south to the upper Meuse (see Figure 2.1), a river in the area of Sedan at the outer edge of the Maginot line, the weakest point in the French front line. Once across the Meuse, Army Group A, with 41,000 vehicles, planned to swing westwards (the cut of the sickle) and thrust to the channel coast, resulting in the encirclement of the bulk of the French forces and their allies. Army Group C, with only 18 divisions, was left to defend the 'Siegfried Line' (a line of defensive forts and tank defences) and launch diversionary attacks on the Maginot Line.

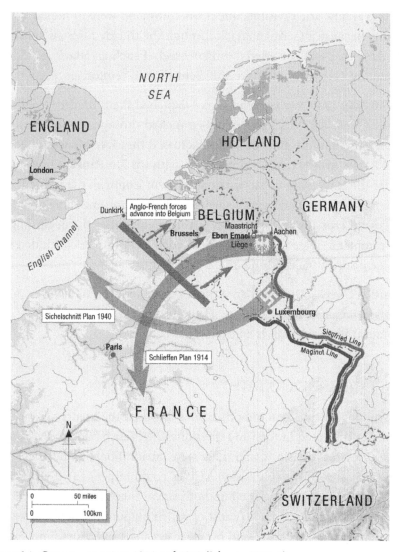

Figure 2.1 *German campaigns 1914 and 1940 (Johnson 2005, 7)*

The French strategy, in contrast, relied on the Dyle Breda plan. The well-equipped Seventh Army, under General Giraud, was placed to the North. In collaboration with the British Expeditionary Force and General Blanchard's First Army, the Allied forces were supposed to move to the River Dyle to absorb the weight of the German attack. General Corap's Ninth Army was to occupy the area along the Meuse just north of Sedan. Below Sedan, holding the gap between Sedan and the start of the Maginot Line, General Huntzinger was placed with his Second Army. The divisions under his command were of mediocre quality because a German attack through the thickly forested area of the Ardennes was considered unlikely and, if such an attack should occur, the French would have sufficient time to reinforce.

On 10 May 1940, the German forces launched their offensive. General Heinz Guderian's XIX Panzer corps punched through the southern end of the Maginot line and successfully crossed the river Meuse at Sedan on 13 May. Meanwhile, General Hoth, with his 7th Panzer Division, under the leadership of the enigmatic Erwin Rommel, overcame the defences at Dinant and established a bridgehead on the same day. The successful crossing of the Meuse, just three days after the beginning of the campaign, sealed the fate of the French Army, to be concluded with the *Armistice* at Compiègne on 22 June 1940.

In just six weeks, the German Armed Forces went on to bring a military juggernaut to its knees. The defeat of the Allies was so profound that it demands an explanation.

DAVID VERSUS GOLIATH

The military disposition of both armies favoured the French. France and her allies mustered in total 134 divisions: the French had 79 divisions plus 13 fortress divisions, and there were an additional 22 Belgian, 10 British and 10 Dutch divisions. Hitler could rely on 135 divisions. In quality, the divisions varied on both sides. The Allies had at their disposal around 3,000 tanks, most of which outgunned their German counterparts (2,400 tanks) and provided greater protection. France also had more artillery pieces than Germany (a ratio of 3 to 2). Only in the air, the allied forces were outclassed by the German Luftwaffe.

Given the allied superiority of arms on the ground, one might be tempted to attribute the defeat to mobile tank warfare, introduced by the Germans. By the same token, the doctrine of armoured *Blitzkrieg* (lightning war) needs to be put in perspective. Only ten German divisions were fully armoured. The majority of the German Forces relied on soldiers on foot, supported by horses. Hence, an armoured lightning war would have been ill-conceived: *'particularly since Guderian's doctrine about tank warfare was neither fully understood nor fully approved by his commanders, and Rommel's idiosyncratic doctrine was at odds with it'* (May 2009, 449). In those cases where the infantry and armour were supported by tactical air support, the impact of the Luftwaffe on the French fortifications can best be described as minimal, especially in the Sedan sector.

The morale of the French Army, especially in the initial stages of the Meuse crossing and despite the later rout, also does not suffice as the primary reason for the ultimate collapse of the front around Sedan. Multiple accounts underline the tenacity and courage with which the French and Belgian defenders along the Meuse opposed the German invaders. In essence, *'whatever the advantages for the Germans, however, the campaign was not a "walk through the sun" for them'* (Doughty 1990, 4).

We need to understand the 'why' of the final outcome, given the setup of a French Goliath versus a German David. How could the Germans have *'outfought the French tactically and outsmarted them strategically'* (Doughty 1990, 4)?

'BATAILLE CONDUITE AND COLMATAGE' VERSUS 'AUFTRAGSTAKTIK'

Let us begin with the overall manner of waging war. France, being reliant on a largely citizen-army, focused predominantly on determining when, where, and how the Germans would attack, and controlling every situation by executing a different plan. The Germans were able to deploy a professional army, although in an ad-hoc fashion. Some planning was carried out, but ultimately, it was down to the 'boots on the ground' to manage a rapidly changing situation, based on the exploitation of human situated cognition – of mindfulness.

From the French perspective, the approach to preventing the Germans from invading their country was predominantly driven by a rule-based approach to managing adversity that was top-down, centralised, and methodical. Encapsulated by the idea of *la bataille conduite* (battle by guidance, or methodical battle), this gave the French forces little freedom to act. With the promise that any attack would be stopped by massive firepower, improvisation was to be avoided, and all steps were meticulously prepared in advance. If the worst happened and the enemy was close to breaking through the French defences, the only French response was to plug (*colmater*) the gap with reinforcements. Their strategic fixation, though, for an operation based on a single scenario assumption left them vulnerable to any unexpected moves by the Germans: '*The French Military knew what kind of war they expected to fight. They also knew where they expected (and wanted) to fight: in Belgium*' (Jackson 2003, 25).

At the heart of the German approach was the autonomous deployment of Panzer forces, relying on the doctrinal approach of *Auftragstaktik* (mission-oriented leadership). Mission-oriented leadership was characterised by the military commanders providing their subordinate leaders with an understanding of the intent behind orders and how these fit into the strategic perspective. Operationally and tactically, these subordinate leaders were equipped with wide-ranging independence and freedom of execution, although within the boundaries of standard operating procedures.

TWO PRINCIPAL MODES OF PROJECT MANAGEMENT REVISITED

The battle of Sedan in May 1940 offers a peculiar picture. If we see it as two project teams in competition, both are equipped with rationales that could guarantee success: '*Thanks largely to an infatuation with a mythical Blitzkrieg, we are far too quick to dismiss the methodical battle as an example of stupid doctrine'* (Kiesling 2003, 114).

Let us move back to the distinction between aleatory and epistemic uncertainty. The French and their Allies adopted a conception of aleatory uncertainty, driven by the Legacy of Victory in WWI (Kutsch 2018, 48). The Germans, in contrast, could not repeat the mistakes of WWI but conceived their upcoming struggle with the French as largely epistemic (Kutsch 2018, 52). As a result, both sides developed distinct coping strategies in line with their conception of uncertainty.

The French High Command rigidly stuck to its plans and its expectations of how these plans would work out. They expected the Germans to attack in the north, through the Low Countries, and so they prepared themselves for the fulfilment of this expectation, constrained by their own capabilities and blind to the capabilities of their enemy.

The Germans displayed an extraordinary wealth of novel ideas on how combat operations should be conducted. These were not just documented as theoretical thought pieces, such as Achtung Panzer (Guderian 1999), originally published in 1937. Visionary ideas were tested in field exercises and war games and further validated in those early campaigns of WWII, such as the invasion of Poland on 1 September 1939 as well as in the campaign against Denmark and Norway of 9 April 1940, a mere four weeks prior to the invasion of France.

The insights gained from these successes and failures – Norway was successfully invaded but at a terrible cost to the German Navy – were heeded despite ongoing conservatism among German generalship. In order to surprise an enemy, the envelope had to be pushed beyond what one knew from past experience. Visionaries took the upper hand.

If there is a criticism about the strategic planning of the Germans, it is that their vision mainly referred to the operational necessity of breaking through the French lines in the Centre and then, through encirclement, demoralising French Forces. Once that aim was accomplished, lack of vision beyond the capitulation of France left a vacuum. At the eve of Operation Yellow's commencement, no vision, let alone any plan, was in place to defeat another enemy: Great Britain.

In contrast to opportunistic thinking, the French strategy was characterised by myopic, out-dated expectations. The campaign in the west in 1940 was preceded by a range of engagements that could have provided the French with an idea of what the Axis forces were capable. Despite these valuable insights, the common belief that 'It cannot happen to us' prevailed. This perception revealed overconfidence in their own plans, which were believed to be so detailed and complete that they would cover all eventualities. Readiness to counter any eventuality other than an attack in the north severely limited their strategic flexibility as prevailing overconfidence was rarely challenged. Concerns about their defences, in particular in the area around Sedan were ignored. Exercises or War Games probing these defences and the readiness of the Allied forces either did not take place or their outcomes were discounted as not applicable to a 'real-life' scenario. In a memorandum written by Colonel Charles de Gaulle, General Keller (Inspector-General of Tanks) pointed out:

> *Even supposing that the present fortified line was breached or outflanked, it does not appear that our opponents will find a combination of circumstances as favourable as Blitzkrieg was in Poland. One can see, then, that in future operations the primary role of the tank will be the same as in the past: to assist the infantry in reaching successive objectives.*

(Horne 1990, 179)

While the Germans did plan, the credo of German commanders was Helmuth von Moltke the Elder's (1800–1891) that no plan survives contact with the enemy. It was a necessity for German commanders to lead from the front and to remain tactically sensitive to an unpredictable, ever-changing situation. Such sensitivity at a tactical level, and its translation into operations and strategy was assisted by the use of wireless communications.

In contrast, French generalship received many situation reports about the unfolding campaign. Communications from the front line arrived frequently, but they were often outdated and ambiguous. Fuelled by overconfidence, reports that indicated a deteriorating situation near Sedan were flatly ignored until the pleas of front-line officers made them 'wake up' to reality; that the front had been broken.

ADAPTABILITY

On some occasions, Allied logistics prevented a timely deployment of forces. At the time when Allied reserves were deployed and on the move, the Germans had already occupied the area in contention, gaining a defensive advantage. On others, French columns of men and material on the move were surprised and subdued by lightly armoured German reconnaissance forces.

The German forces showed greater adaptability, facilitated by tactical sensitivity and logistical independence. A common pattern emerged in this campaign: one of quick action in line with tactical and operational necessities, but still in line with strategic foresight. In essence, German planning allowed and encouraged forms of improvisation, an extreme form of adaptability. Its purpose is to create and maintain uncertainty and ambiguity for the enemy to such an extent that he is incapable of adapting to circumstances (adapted from Kutsch 2018, 59–61).

Overall, these two coping strategies, synthesised as French rule-based versus German mindfulness-based, are fundamentally different styles and both offer advantages that, in the light of the superior resources on the French side, should not have allowed the breakthrough at Sedan. Nevertheless, as with any project, the question is less about the critical resources than how they are applied in practice and how they are utilised to meet the overall objective. Regarding the application of rule-based and mindfulness-based project management, let us consider:

- Time – What is the effect of time on processes, functioning, behaviour and performance?
- Team – How do groups of people in temporary organisational systems resolve issues of uncertainty and risk?
- Task – What kind of tasks do temporary organisational forms perform?

TIME

How did the French make sense of time? Their approach to engaging with the upcoming German attack was set by prior expectations. These expectations and the planning that went with them added to a form of 'tunnel vision', a restricted understanding that the Germans would attack through Belgium. Alternative frames of reality were blocked out, despite ongoing concerns about the unpreparedness of the Sedan front. Once the offensive was underway, the French generals were not sufficiently close to operations to realise in realtime that their plans did not apply to the situation at hand:

> *Gamelin's headquarters were as far back as Vincennes, virtually in the Paris suburbs, because the Commander-in-Chief felt he needed to be closer to the Government than to his own Army. His field commander, Alphonse Georges ... was based in La Ferte, 35 miles east of Paris, but spent much of his time at his residence 12 miles from the capital.*

(Roberts 2009, 56)

Crucial information that came to the attention of the French High Command was already out of date upon their receiving it, at times by several hours. Even when they did receive information, they failed to see that anything was going awry. This was typified by reports they received from the front, massively underestimating the situation. For example, General Huntzinger's staff reported: *'There has been a rather serious hitch at Sedan'*.

This situation report offers an insight into the self-inflicted state of mindlessness, as a form of deception and denial. Information about successes, for example against the 2nd Panzer Division which was struggling to reach its staging area on time and was bogged down by French artillery, was amplified. In contrast, information about retreats, initially carried out in a planned and methodical way, was downplayed to the extent that Georges signalled Gamelin at midnight on 13 May: *'Here we are all calm'* (May 2009, 411).

The French mindless fixation on a single theatre of battle in the north, lack of sensitivity to the state of defence in the Sedan sector and being cut off from information, coupled with ignorance and the premature commitment of reserves based on expectations, meant that, for the Allies, the battle for France was fought in something of a vacuum. Only the opportunistic intervention of individual divisions could have turned the tide. However, bound by a top-down approach, decisions to counterattack were taken late or not at all. Furthermore, where opportunities emerged to counter the establishment of a German bridgehead, logistical dependencies prevented a quick reaction. For example, the mobilisation of counterattacks by the 55th Division, which was responsible for the Sedan sector, was bogged down by the layers of hierarchy through which orders had to find their way. It took a staggering nine hours to mobilise a counterattack. By then, the situation on the ground had already changed considerably:

1900 hours: Telephone discussion between Grandsard and Lafontaine about attachment of additional infantry and tanks for a counterattack.

1930 hours: Telephone discussion between Grandsard and Lafontaine about moving command post of 55th Division.

After 1930 hours: Movement of 55th's command post. Lafontaine meets Labarthe in Chemery.

After 1930 hours: Lieutenant Colonel Cachou, who was the deputy Chief of Staff of the Xth Corps, meets Labarthe in Chemery. Approves Labarthe's decision not to move north.

After 1930 hours: Cachou meets Lafontaine east of Chemery. Informs him of Labarthe's decision.

After 1930 hours: Lafontaine calls Grandsard to discuss counterattack.

2200–2300 hours: Lafontaine learns that the 205th Regiment and 4th Tank Battalion are being attached to the 55th Division.

2400 hours: Lafontaine departs for Xth Corps command post.

0130 hours: Chaligne learns that counterattack would consist of two infantry regiments and two tank battalions.

0300 hours: Lafontaine returns to Chemery without having reached Xth Corps.

0415 hours: Lafontaine issues an order for counterattack (Doughty 1990, 260).

The well-prepared plans gave a false impression of what was expected to be happening and when. Events were expected to unfold as the plan predicted, yet what was happening in the field told a different story. The discrepancy between expectations and reality could not readily be compensated for as real-time updates were either downplayed or took too long to be relayed between the commanders and the front line.

In contrast, the Germans considered time as organic. Their strategic planning for the invasion of France was superseded by the operational necessities and uncertainties. A river needs to be crossed quickly, no matter what, as everything else depends on its outcome. This may sound haphazard and reckless, but detailed planning of the 'when' and 'how' was replaced by 'whatever' was operationally necessary, given the unfolding events on the ground – the initially conceived plan of 'what should be done when' was no longer the overriding factor. Instead, mindful responses 'in the moment' meant that timely decisions and actions were paramount; all in light of the strategic intent to breach the French front at a place where the French would expect it the least.

TEAM

The French doctrine was characterised by centralised, hierarchical, decision-making. This is unsurprising given that those executing orders – mostly conscripts – had little or no experience and were given only limited training to make decisions on their own. As team members were often allocated to areas of operation and to regiments they were unfamiliar with, there was little social bonding and familiarity about their environment prevailed. Such inconsistency is often associated with modern projects, in which resources are parachuted in for a limited period, initially oblivious of context. The teams – platoons, regiments, and battalions – were expected to function by following the orders provided, context-free. This is the classic mindless 'command and control' style. Orders were stripped of the 'why', and this could not be replaced by the (lack of) experience of those that had to execute them.

The German approach, in stark contrast, focused on the development of internally cohesive, well-equipped teams with an extraordinary response repository and independence to exercise flexibility in action. Subordinate leaders were given, in no small extent, insights into the mission objectives and strategic ramifications, and freedom in execution. For example, General Heinz Guderian (XIXth Panzer Corps, Sedan) later reflected:

> During the French campaign, I never received any further orders as to what I was to do once the bridgehead over the Meuse was captured. All of my decisions, until I reached the Atlantic seaboard at Abbeville, were taken by me alone.

> (Guderian 2000, 251)

Before Operation Yellow, teams of specialists were defined within Panzergruppe Kleist. They were kept together as much as possible and rehearsed a range of scenarios, ranging from amphibious landings to urban warfare. These kinds of 'Tiger Teams' were given the experience of the context of warfare through rehearsals, and their performance was driven by orders from superiors who were very 'close' to them. Officers such as Guderian and Rommel 'led from the front', capturing time as it unfolded, racing between their headquarters and the developing events. Rommel, for example, tried to be always in the 'picture' of developing events by crossing the Meuse with one of the first waves of assault teams. His scepticism about initial success turned into a curiosity about what was going on.

TASK

The French front-line soldiers were tasked with countering a German attack. However, using the example of the 147th Division, their preparations included constant digging and fortifying, with little emphasis on the practical aspects of combat: '*Many of the soldiers in the 147th knew their responsibilities in the smallest detail, but their skills for defending fortresses or firing machine guns were useless in regular infantry units*' (Doughty 1990, 127).

Their preparation – digging and fortifying – left little time to prepare the French soldiers for actual fighting. It was – wrongly – assumed that giving orders to the front-line soldiers would compensate for the lack of knowing 'why' and 'how'. Execution of tasks was expected to be done in isolation of the specific context. This would not have been such a problem if the orders matched the unfolding situation. Unfortunately, that was not the case and backed into a corner with orders that no longer made sense, the French Forces took their initiative and retreated in the hope of receiving fresh orders to form another coherent front further back.

With the French very much rule- and task-oriented, the Germans followed a slightly different approach of goal-orientation, in which the achievements of objectives superseded the specificity of execution. Such goal-orientation can only work if teams are prepared and ready to carry out any task necessary to accomplish the given aims. Their flexibility was such that not only did they provide their logistics, but they also made sure that a range of specialists (e.g. the *Grossdeutschland* Regiment) were immediately available to adapt to a changing situation.

The German forces applied a potentially costly strategy of mindfulness. With speed as the essential factor, the crossing of the Meuse received operational preference. Such intent was carried out with a specialised, yet operationally and logistically independent, force. Methodology and operating procedures – rule-based management – played less of a role because of the specially trained units' ability to achieve the intent of crossing a river and establishing a bridgehead. This subsequently enabled the encirclement of the French Forces, and this logic was embedded in their thinking. Rules did not have to be tightly controlled, and deviation from a method for the benefit of achieving the operational aim was not only allowed but encouraged.

The French followed a supposedly more certain strategy of not allowing French front-line soldiers and officers to mindfully think on their feet. Orders were relayed from the top to the front line, to be executed without question. This does make sense given the largely conscript army whose soldiers would not have the knowledge and experience to think and act flexibly enough under such severe conditions. The ultimate breakdown of the rule-based approach here was down to delayed or absent communication and the lack of preparation for the scenario that unfolded.

> *More than anything else, this happened because France and its allies misjudged what Germany planned to do. If leaders in the Allied governments had anticipated the German offensive through the Ardennes, even as a worrisome contingency, it is almost inconceivable that France would have been defeated when and as it was. It is more conceivable that the outcome would have been not France's defeat but Germany's and, possibly, a French victory parade on the Unter den Linden in Berlin.*
>
> (May 2009, 5)

THE TEMPTATION OF RULE-BASED PROJECT MANAGEMENT

On the one hand, a rule-based approach to project management offers greater efficiency, accountability and stability (or, perhaps, the illusion of it). On the other hand, a situated cognition-based approach to epistemic uncertainty provides the required flexibility to deal with situations that deviate from the norm. And there is the problem. In projects, we often start with a rule-based approach, as the French did. We plan, set up procedures and run our projects the 'right' way. It is a form of 'dogmatism', the tendency to lay down principles as incontrovertibly 'true', without consideration of the evidence or the opinions of others.

Such dogmatism, developed over time, may undermine readiness to address epistemic uncertainty. Why communicate extensively if a planned future of normality is assumed? Such dogmatism is entrenched by long periods of planning and the absence of failure. This sends the message that the system is working, reinforcing faith in the process. The more we believe that plans will unfold as predicted, relying on an expectation of aleatoric uncertainty, the less we prepare and ready ourselves for epistemic uncertainty: for a situation that unfolds beyond the risk horizon. It is not surprising that the French held on to their planned expectations until it was too late.

Even the Germans, after their stunning success in overcoming their French foe in May/June 1940, they encountered a practical drift in the following years towards a rule-based form of management:

> *The rapidity of the German victory [in France] had created a dangerous hubris among the German military and on the part of Hitler himself a fatal conviction that he was a military genius who could never be wrong. This was to prove his ultimate undoing.*
>
> (Jackson 2003, 237)

A stark example of this practical drift was the battle of Kursk in July–August 1943. Hitler gave his generals little leeway in planning this battle and what they produced was a transparent scheme that the Senior Soviet planners easily anticipated. Imagination played a lesser role. The focus on the repetition of previous schemes of warfare, the obsession of Hitler to plan every move in detail – similar to the French in 1940 – and the constant delay in launching the offensive (e.g. because of the deployment of new tank designs) turned the battle of Kursk into a methodical and inflexible endeavour that was countered by the Soviet Union even before it started. As a result, after Kursk, initiative changed hands at Kursk, and the defeat of Nazi Germany was accelerated by the lack of manpower and as well as an increasingly centralised, rule-based approach to decision-making by the German High Command and Hitler:

> *It was one of the great ironies of the War that as Hitler, frustrated and disillusioned from being unable to secure victory over the USSR proceeded to deprive his commanders of their independence and centralized more and more the conduct of the war into his own hands, Stalin was moving in the opposite direction, seeking*

to encourage within the Red Army that very operational flexibility
and independence in decision-making in the field that had been
responsible for Germany's victories in the first three years of
the conflict.

(Healy 2008, 109)

In projects, the question is not whether to adopt a fully rule-based or mindfulness-based approach, because they both have their advantages and disadvantages. We often see projects being set up with a rule-based approach, or to shift gradually to one characterised by reducing situated human cognition and a greater focus on compliance with rules and procedures. Does that automatically imply that this approach is superior, despite the inability of the French Forces to make it work in 1940? Well, yes and no. Rule-based management is a more fruitful approach in environments that unfold very much in linear, predictable ways, informed by aleatoric uncertainty; so, by default, environments that do not favour project management in the first place, but rather operations management.

MINDFULNESS AND PROJECT MANAGEMENT

Standards in project management are various. Most dominant are those of the Project Management Institute (PMI), the UK Government Centre for Information Systems and the British Standards Institution, all of which offer similar, if not identical, standards for project management. Those advocated by the PMI are widely used and are considered to be a competency standard. The PMI standard *A Guide to the Project Management Body of Knowledge* (PMBOK) includes nine areas of project management knowledge: project integration management, project scope management, project time management, project cost management, project quality management, project communications management, project risk management and project procurement management.

The purpose of project management is seen as the management of entities such as tasks, requirements and objectives in advance, and is reliant on hindsight as a predictor for future changes. However, the problem that project management faces relates to the degree of uncertainty that is inherent in a project. This problem, arising through the lack of hindsight, means that project managers may not rely on the validity of probabilistic estimates grounded in historical data.

The PMBOK guide approach to 'best' practice project management standards, as introduced and promoted by organisations such as PMI or APM, is advocated as being self-evidently correct. In this respect, Williams (2005, 2) argues:

> *Project management as set out in this work is presented as a set of procedures that are self-evidently correct: following these procedures will produce effectively managed projects; project failure is indicative of inadequate attention to the project management procedures.*

Modern project management bodies of knowledge tend to assume a world of aleatoric uncertainty (or in other words, risks) where past occurrences can inform the future. The underlying rationale is that risk can be 'designed out' of a project by probabilistic, deterministic planning tools, enforced and applied consistently. Epistemic uncertainty plays a much smaller part in this logic. At the centre of such rule-based project management is the pre-loading and automation of fixed responses, based on a past-informed future. A rule-based approach is fundamentally Taylorist, breaking every project action, job, or task into small and simple segments which can be easily analysed and efficiently delivered. Rules are put in place to pre-plan the future-based actions of forecasting, assessing and scheduling with the express purpose of prevention, embodied in project management tools like PERT, network planning and earned value analysis. Human cognition – as a potential source of error – is being replaced by these pre-planned and pre-loaded actions. A benefit of this approach is the consistency of action (and we do fully acknowledge the benefits), but they are not without limitations. An 'autopilot' may enable managers to deal with common problems quickly and consistently but may struggle with effective responses to novelty and ambiguity.

That highlights again the uneasy coexistence between professional bodies of knowledge and the validation, but also criticism, from their research counterparts. In essence, the fundamental assumption of traditional project management standards is that the project is decoupled from its environment. That is to say, once the project is planned, changes should happen only occasionally. Assumptions of project management include knowledge of probable future states and repeatability of event, and at its foremost, decision-makers free of cognitive errors.

Nevertheless, none of us can possibly claim to be free of cognitive biases that cloud our thinking about managing a project. Cognitive failures are best understood in the context of how our minds operate. In principle, intuitive processes define hard-wired routines, informed by experiences, that enable us to engage with daily occurrences, such as driving a car repeatedly from and to work. The successions of routines are an expression of mindless, rule-based behaviour:

> So often in our lives, we act as though there were only one set of rules. For instance, in cooking, we tend to follow recipes with dutiful precision. We add ingredients as though by official decree. If the recipe calls for a pinch of salt and four pinches fall in, panic strikes, as though the bowl might now explode. Thinking of a recipe only as a rule, we often do not consider how people tastes vary, or what fun it might be to make up a new dish.

> (Langer 1989, 16)

Analytic processes break into our propensity to adhere to routines, rules, processes and procedures. They are conscious, deliberate, and define our state of increased awareness of our surroundings as a stepping stone to mindfully engage with adversity such as uncertainty and complexity.

It is these analytic processes that self-evidently correct project management does not address. One may even claim that pursuit of ever greater compliance to past-informed rules, processes and techniques (such as probabilistic risk management) undermines our ability to trigger analytic processes of thinking and reduces our ability to maintain a state of mindful being and thinking. In this respect, it is worth noting that project management frameworks (even Agile Project Management) 'just' want to do that: automating past-informed actions.

But Mindfulness can help us to fight the tendency to fall prey to intuitive processes (Denyer et al. 2011), to counter the urge to routinise and thus automate our actions in a project. Project Management should be anything but past-informed. By default, projects are volatile, uncertain, complex and ambiguous. As a result, mindful practices are part of a debiasing strategy, a capacity to override intuitive processes.

We are not the first to write about rule-based versus mindfulness-based approaches in organisations or projects. For further reading, there are a range of books that we saw as central in writing this synthesis:

- Weick, Karl, and Kathleen Sutcliffe, 2015. *Managing the Unexpected: Sustained Performance in a Complex World* (Weick and Sutcliffe 2015): This book builds on the pioneering work of a concept called High-Reliability Organisations. It offers a compelling insight into a variety of disasters and provides practical advice on how to establish and maintain a state of collective mindfulness for reliable and resilient performance.

- Snook, Scott A., *Friendly Fire: The Accidental Shootdown of US Black Hawks over Northern Iraq* (Snook 2000): Snook delves into a 'blue-on-blue' incident in the No-Fly Zone over Iraq in 1994, with the loss of 26 military personnel. He provides a fascinating account of the events leading to that fateful shootdown. He avoids the definition of a root cause but acknowledges that the combination of a multitude of behavioural factors led to this disaster. His analysis is contextual such that it makes generalisation beyond that incident difficult, but it encourages readers to appreciate the complexity and thus the difficulty of preventing incidents like this from happening again. Snook's major contribution was the theory of Practical Drift, which does seem to be more widely applicable.

- Perrow, Charles, *Normal Accidents* (Perrow 1999): This book could be interpreted as saying that accidents are bound to happen due to the complexity and uncertainty inherent in an environment. They are hence 'normal'. Perrow offers insights into a variety of disasters, including the role of people as a contributing factor. He categorises industries according to 'coupling' and 'interactions', and so offers an interesting take on how vulnerable each industry is to a 'normal accident'. One may argue that, in Perrow's view, the glass is half-empty, whereas, with Weick, it is half-full. It is an excellent counterargument to Weick and Sutcliffe's book on High-Reliability Organisations, although with similarities in content.

- Reason, James, *The Human Contribution: Unsafe Acts, Accidents and Heroic Recoveries* (Reason 2008): This is probably the most updated account of human situated cognition. Reason captures the audience through his style of writing as well as his in-depth insight into the complexity of the human mind but tells us that there is a way of enabling systems to be more resilient.

- Langer, Ellen, *Mindfulness* (Langer 1989): One might consider this book as the foundation for many of those previously mentioned on mindfulness, a critical angle in this book. If you would like to explore your resilience, this book is a good start. Langer offers four dimensions of individual mindfulness:
- Novelty seeking: The propensity to explore and engage with novel stimuli. This refers to a tendency to perceive every situation as 'new'. This type of person is likely to be more interested in experiencing a variety of stimuli, rather than mastering a specific situation.
- Novelty producing: The propensity to develop new ideas and ways of looking at things.
- Engagement: The propensity to become involved in any given situation. An individual who scores high in engagement is likely to see the 'big picture'.
- Flexibility: The flexible individual believes in the fluidity of information and the importance of welcoming a changing environment rather than resisting it. Flexibility, in this case, refers to someone who can view a situation from multiple perspectives and recognise that each aspect has equal value.

TOWARDS MINDFULNESS-BASED PROJECT MANAGEMENT

A mindfulness-based approach is more suited to managing projects characterised by epistemic uncertainty. The significant benefit of this as a management approach is that it provides greater awareness, a more nuanced appreciation of changing circumstances and greater flexibility in containing epistemic uncertainty. Rules are ill-suited to deal with novelty and ambiguity. Not so, our minds. As flawed as they may be, they offer fantastic flexibility to deal with uncertainty, a feat no rule-based system can ever achieve.

What many managers have failed to appreciate is that human variability offers a way of providing the flexibility necessary to manage epistemic uncertainty. It is increasingly recognised that a broader perspective on dealing with uncertainty is required if one wants to look beyond what has repeatedly happened in the past. This has led to an acknowledgement that rule-based management is beneficial, as long as it allows mindfulness to flourish. 'True' resilience in a project is most likely the outcome of some rule-based control, yet with leeway to deploy the human mind to accommodate epistemic uncertainty.

Consequently, in most successful modern projects, one can find a mix of both rule-based and mindfulness-based approaches to managing risk and uncertainty (see Chapter 8). It is the ability to impose control, yet offer enough 'space' to mindfully manage the uncertainty that goes beyond what one can predict and plan for in detail. Furthermore, resilient projects are those in which the project manager and team are reluctant – in the absence of failure or because of failure – to give in to the temptation to impose ever more adherence to plans, implemented in a rule-based manner. The following chapters go into more detail on what obstacles we may need to overcome to be mindful so that we can ready and prepare ourselves better for epistemic uncertainty.

REFERENCES

Denyer, D., E. Kutsch, E. (Liz) Lee-Kelley, and M. Hall. 2011. "Exploring Reliability in Information Systems Programmes." *International Journal of Project Management* 29(4): 442–54.

Doughty, R A. 1990. *The Breaking Point: Sedan and the Fall of France*. Hamden: Archon.

Guderian, H. 1999. *Achtung Panzer!*. London: Cassell.

———. 2000. *Panzer Leader*. London: Penguin Classics.

Healy, M. 2008. *Zitadelle: The German Offensive against the Kursk Salient 4–17 July 1943*. Cheltenham: The History Press.

Horne, A. 1990. *To Lose a Battle: France 1940*. London: Penguin Books.

Jackson, J. 2003. *The Fall of France*. New York: Oxford University Press.

Johnson, H. 2005. *Fort Eben Emael: The Key to Hitler's Victory in the West*. Oxford: Osprey Publishing.

Kiesling, E. C. 2003. "The Fall of France: Lessons of the 1940 Campaign." *Defence Studies* 3(1): 109–23.

Kutsch, E. 2018. *The Art of Organisational Resilience: Revisiting the Fall of France in 1940*. Abington: Routledge.

Langer, E. 1989. *Mindfulness*. Cambridge: Perseus Publishing.

May, E. 2009. *Strange Victory: Hitler's Conquest of France*. London: I.B. Tauris & Co.

Perrow, C. 1999. *Normal Accidents: Living with High-Risk Technologies*. Princeton NJ: Princeton University Press.

Reason, J. 2008. *The Human Contribution: Unsafe Acts, Accidents and Heroic Recoveries*. Boca Raton: Taylor & Francis.

Roberts, A. 2009. *The Storm of War: A New History of the Second World War*. London: Penguin.

Snook, S. A. 2000. *Friendly Fire – the Accidental Shootdown of U.S. Black Hawks over Northern Iraq*. Princeton, NJ: Princeton University Press.

Weick, K., and K. Sutcliffe. 2015. *Managing the Unexpected: Sustained Performance in a Complex World*, 3rd ed. Hoboken, NJ: Wiley.

Williams, T. 2005. "Assessing and Moving on from the Dominant Project Management Discourse in the Light of Project Overruns." *IEEE Transactions on Engineering Management* 52(4): 497–508.

CHAPTER THREE

The art of noticing

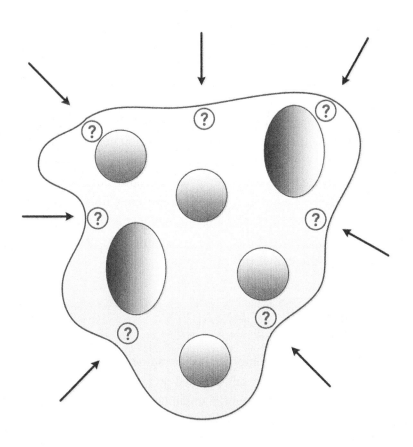

CONTENTS

A project team may well find itself facing the challenge of epistemic uncertainty. The lead-up to this can be ambiguous and subtle, and often there is little warning. It is useful to foster a keen state of awareness that recognises and anticipates emerging adversity. This chapter provides some answers as to how epistemic uncertainty can be noticed, if not necessarily forecast traditionally. It addresses the issue of how we can notice more about those events impacting our project to which we have little knowledge of.

THE LURE OF NORMALITY

On our road to 'notice more', there are some obstacles. A central challenge is somewhat self-inflicted and lies with our way of thinking. We are naturally tempted to fall back on our ideas of a world of normality because we tend to feel more comfortable with that; there is a range of lures that limit our noticing.

EXPECTATIONS OF NORMALITY

We want things to be fine. We would like the plan to unfold just as the schedule pinned to the wall shows that it should. We long for a continuous state of normality and therefore perhaps it is not surprising that such longings lead us to ignore indications of future failure. We may be surrounded by signs of potential adversity, yet because these do not fit our expectations, we tend to disregard them so that our stakeholders and we remain in a state of relative comfort.

NORMALCY BIAS

In 79 AD, Mount Vesuvius, an active volcano just south of modern-day Naples in Italy, erupted burying the Roman city of Pompeii. In hindsight, the 16,000 inhabitants may well have survived if they had not spent hours watching the eruption until it was too late to escape. This lesson from history is an example of normalcy bias, or normality bias (more colloquially referred to as the incredulity response, and, most interesting of all, the ostrich effect). Normalcy bias can be defined as the tendency of people to minimise the probability of potential threats or their dangerous implications (Perry et al. 1982). Even when there is a certainty of disaster, people exhibiting normalcy bias will await confirmation from other sources (or just watch whatever everyone else is doing) before taking any kind of action (Omer and Alon 1994). As in Pompeii, people tend to underestimate the likelihood of a disaster and its possible effects and do not take action until it is too late. Essentially, it is the assumption that nothing bad will happen in the future because nothing bad has happened in the past.

Virtually every major disaster in history had some element of normalcy bias as a component. Because there have been years of safety in a city does not mean that it will never be targeted by terrorists. Because previous hurricanes have not caused major disaster does not mean that future ones will be equally benign, as Hurricane Sandy and Hurricane Katrina demonstrated. In the face of natural or other major disasters, the temptation is to blame government inaction, but even where there are preparations in place, people are often inactive until it is too late.

Normalcy bias can frequently be seen in business environments before some major business disaster. Eric Brown, the technology consultant, investor, and entrepreneur recounts how, when he worked at WorldCom in the 1990s, the company was experiencing dramatic growth and fantastic profits. He observes that everyone could see that this was unsustainable and that the organisation was going to implode at some point soon, but nobody was taking steps to tackle the problems in the company, or even trying to identify the problems. Brown notes that people were saying that nothing had happened yet so they doubted anything would happen any time soon. In 2002, WorldCom filed for, at that time, the largest bankruptcy ever. There were lots of reasons for people to be concerned about their operations and the business model but instead of trying to tackle these concerns people ignored them. Normalcy bias is a danger to organisations because people assuming everything is going to be all right will fail to plan for problems that might beset their organisation.

That said, normalcy bias is a perfectly natural behaviour. Psychological studies have found that about 70 per cent of people are affected by normalcy bias and that, in many cases, this is a good thing because it helps to pacify the other 30 per cent who are prone to over-reacting and losing control. However, the problem with this is that they also hinder those who are doing the right thing.

COMPLACENCY

The assumption of normality is reinforced by periods of success. Success is characterised by the absence of failures. Such accomplishments in the past make us think that we can expect the same to continue. We are increasingly focused on what has worked, rather than on what might go wrong. Hence, we may limit our attention with regards to signs of possible failure. Our minds are focused on what we want to see. We anticipate that this success will continue and any potential signs of looming adversity do not fit our expectations. This complacency means that we are more attentive to information that reinforces our confidence and less likely to pick up on small signs of trouble ahead.

HINDSIGHT BIAS

Another bias related to cognitive psychology is hindsight bias, also known as the knew-it-all-along effect or creeping determinism (Roese and Vohs 2012). It is a tendency to see an event as having been predictable after the event, despite there having been little or no objective basis for predicting it. It is one of the most widely studied 'decision traps', with studies ranging from sports results and medical diagnoses to political strategy, including accountancy and business decisions. It results in people believing that events were more predictable than they were in reality, which can result in an oversimplification of cause and effect.

In organisation studies, hindsight bias is very frequently cited (Christensen-Szalanski and Beach 2006). The effects of hindsight bias are that people tend to overestimate the quality of their decision-making, where the results were positive, and underestimate the quality of decisions where the results were negative. For example, if a student drops out of a prestigious university and then goes on to found a multi-billion dollar company, the decision might appear to be far more intelligent than it is. Another effect is to see innovations from the past as far less inventive than they were as they become obvious in hindsight. A very common example is for people to overestimate their foreknowledge of an event. For example, traders may think they know a crash is coming every week for years in advance of the stock market crash coming. When the crash comes, traders conclude they 'knew it all along'. The result is that individuals have overconfidence and begin to overestimate their insight and talent and possibly believe they can predict the future with some kind of accuracy. Another effect is sometimes known as 'chronological snobbery'. People of the past are viewed as ignorant and irrational, and the effect is that people do not believe they can learn much from people of the past. Another effect of hindsight bias is that people do not plan or prepare adequately or collect sufficient information and data as this effort is regarded as a waste of time as last time they put the effort in, the result was one they 'knew all about' anyway.

There are three levels of hindsight bias (Roese and Vohs 2012):

- Memory distortion, which involves misremembering an earlier opinion or judgment. People selectively recall information that confirms what they already knew to be true. As they look back on their earlier predictions, they tend to believe that they did know the answer all along.
- Inevitability, centres on people's beliefs that the event was inevitable. People try to create a narrative that makes sense of the information they have.
- Foreseeability, involves the belief that people personally could have foreseen an event. People interpret that to mean that the outcome must have been foreseeable from the beginning.

FOCUSING ON THE FAMILIAR

Even so, some of the messages may make it onto our 'radar' of noticing. We are more likely to take into account the information we are familiar with. For example, if a potential problem looks similar to one we have encountered in the past, this familiarity helps us identify and make sense of it. Consequently, our attention may be drawn to those factors we are more accustomed to. Unfamiliar features, amplified by ambiguity, are more likely to be filtered from our attention.

AIMING AT THE MEASURABLE

Filtering out the unfamiliar failures goes hand-in-hand with paying attention to the measurable and quantifiable. If a piece of information lacks specificity, we tend to blank it out. Hence, we might only take into consideration information about a failure that is unambiguous enough to be processed. Further, that is to say, to be managed. As a consequence, we might take our project into the unknown, only noticing or wanting to notice aspects of failure that are 'clear' enough to us and that we have experienced in the past. However, because we have a tendency only to notice what we expect to notice, our 'radar', especially for uncertainty, is often not as sensitive as we would like.

NEGATIVE CONNOTATION

The term 'risk' (or aleatory uncertainty) is often understood as 'bad things happening'. The upside, 'opportunity', is far less commonly discussed. Who would believe adversity to be a 'good' thing? These negative connotations frame the discussion in a bad light, as the language used hints at the manager's inability to design all adversity out of a project in the first place. Overweighting the 'bad' in projects make us lose sight of opportunities.

OBSERVATIONAL SELECTION BIAS

Observational selection bias is the effect of suddenly noticing things that were not previously noticed and, as a result, wrongly assuming that the frequency has increased. The things we notice are not more common than they were before; we just are noticing them more. The problem with selection bias of this nature is that if the sample we observe is not a representative one, our resulting judgments can be seriously flawed (Denrell 2005).

A good example is to seek to identify the ways to do successful business by studying only existing successful businesses. It is a classic statistical trap of drawing conclusions from unrepresentative samples. Without also looking at unsuccessful businesses, people might privilege risky business practices, seeing only those companies that succeeded by adopting those practices and not seeing the ones who failed.

A classic case illustrates both how selection bias created problems and how it could be overcome. During WWII, a Jewish Hungarian mathematician, Abraham Wald (who had emigrated to the United States to escape Nazi Germany), was asked to look at the survivability of bombers. Aircraft that had returned had been badly damaged. Aircraft designers had added extra armour to parts of the aircraft that had been most badly damaged but this had not improved survivability and, in fact, losses had increased as the aircraft were now less agile. Wald reasoned that the aircraft that had returned were the survivors and instructed that the extra armour should be added to the undamaged parts. The surviving aircraft showed where non-lethal damage had been inflicted. The result was an increase in aircraft surviving bombing runs (Ellenberg 2015). This case illustrates how the aircraft designers were basing their decisions on a biased sample and how Wald understood that the correct sample was not even observable.

There are many ways in which managers in businesses base their decisions on biased selections. These include biased samples, either through self-selection or from drawing conclusions from too small a sample (often drawing conclusions from a sample of one!). Often, managers will dredge data or cherry-pick examples that prove their preconception.

Ultimately, managers are advised to beware of basing their decisions of very limited or biased samples. This can, in particular, impact risk-taking (Denrell 2003) as managers may well miss early warning signs of emerging risk or even misinterpret signs of problems as meaning that things are going fine.

ZOOMING IN

When we are preoccupied with 'doing things', our capacity to look out for new signs of adversity is diminished. When we are fixated on – preoccupied with – what matters to us, we tend to lose the ability to detect other important information. Early detection of fixation is highly beneficial. In the aftermath of materialised uncertainty, even with the benefit of hindsight, we may not understand how we didn't recognise the signs of impending difficulty.

MYOPIA

A fixation on getting things done, our expectation of normality and our focus on the tangible and measurable leads to a propensity to be 'short-sighted' – to look into the near future and ignore long-term scenarios. We may only consider the short-term future, leaving us unprepared for what could lie beyond our risk horizon.

TEMPORAL DISCOUNTING

Also known as time discounting or hyperbolic discounting, temporal discounting describes the tendency for people to seek instant gratification. They will choose a reward in the here-and-now rather than the prospect of a greater reward sometime in the future; and, the further into the future the reward is, the lower the value attributed to it. Temporal discounting leads us to downplay the future negative consequences of decisions that have positive consequences right now, and it helps explain why we tend to focus on the immediate consequences of an action without fully considering its long-term effects. It is often referred to as hyperbolic discounting as the effect can be shown as a hyperbola (as opposed to exponential) curve over time. In other words, for any option, when a certain time threshold is passed, the devaluing effect of time diminishes.

Neuroscience has discovered that people's brains are geared to maximising rewards (Haith et al. 2012), which means we have a desire for greater satisfaction in the present. This means that we do not reason things through but make discounting decisions reflexively and automatically. This creates significant problems for businesses and helps to explain why so many companies avoid fixing problems until they are forced to, and why so many companies, and investors emphasise near-term success over long-term profitability. It also helps to explain the phenomena as varied as to why people do not save for pensions, why people struggle to lose weight, and why they have problems with alcohol and substance abuse.

KEY ENABLERS TO THE ART OF NOTICING

In the previous section, we identified some of the behavioural shortcomings that limit our ability to notice, in particular, epistemic uncertainty. There is help, though! In the following sections, we provide an overview of 'what' one can do and 'how'. We elaborate on how to notice and, in particular, how to detect signs of adversity which lack the specificity of risk. The key issue of noticing is – traditionally – one of living in the past and believing that the future will unfold as the past did. Worse, in the absence of failure, we gradually reduce our awareness of the need to 'look out' for warning signs that are unfamiliar and immeasurable, yet which could provide us with an early warning that something is not right. So what does this mean in practice for the project manager?

ACKNOWLEDGEMENT

To notice indications of epistemic uncertainty, one needs to understand the environment that is at stake: the project. Noticing epistemic uncertainty without knowledge about the human, technical, organisational, and environmental factors that determine the success of a project is comparable to trying to find a needle in a haystack without understanding the concept of a haystack. Therein lies the challenge. Projects are inherently uncertain and complex. Any understanding of 'how it works' might be temporary, at best, and necessitates a knowledge of the project 'here-and-now' as well as the needs and wants of the multiple stakeholders.

So the first enabler of greater resilience is an acknowledgement that our world is uncertain; it is a message of 'we do not necessarily know' that is powerful and yet often unnerving, as it counters our longing for certainty and comfort.

VIGILANCE

Accepting this knowledge deficiency and the resulting epistemic uncertainty should trigger an almost permanent state of unease. This unease stems from the project constantly being assailed by uncertainty: every new action and activity is an opportunity for something to go wrong or to work out unexpectedly. This is not, though, a reason for project participants to panic. Rather, it is a reason to be alert and attuned to the possibility that any minor error, problem, or close call could be symptomatic of a flaw in the wider project system. Such events must be scrutinised with the 'big picture' in mind. What may be the possible wider implications?

This means that the process of anticipation should never really cease, but ought to manifest itself in the project environment. This should result in heightened alertness for the project manager and the team. They must be alive to the vagaries of the project, not just in terms of variances in the overall schedule and budget but also in terms of the wider project system and its multiple interconnected aspects.

FREEDOM TO BE VIGILANT

This sense of unease and the alertness to the signs of materialising uncertainty should not come out of thin air. What is required is 'space' in the form of time to spend on spotting failure. Project managers who are preoccupied with administrative tasks may be less sensitive to any failure happening around them. They need to be given the freedom and opportunity to be on the lookout – permanently – and to ask potentially inconvenient questions. This involves spending time close to what is happening. This is often not what we see project managers doing. Sometimes, organisational incentives and systems drive managers to focus on detailed reporting and ensuring adherence to the original plan. This is all well and good, of course, but execution with only limited alertness is like crossing a busy street with only one eye on the traffic.

REPORTING CULTURE

It is not just down to the project manager to be on high alert. Emerging uncertainty should be spotted throughout the project by the various participants. To create effective project awareness, though, warning signs of impending adversity needs to be reported quickly and honestly. Organisational culture (and the lack of incentives) often means that 'bad news' is not passed on to others. Silo thinking and the negative connotations of such 'inconveniences' can prevent people from reporting failures, both small and large. When adversity strikes or individuals suspect poor performance, they need to share this information confidently and promptly, without the fear of being blamed or considered a troublemaker.

CROSS-FUNCTIONAL TEAMS

Projects are best run with the benefit of multiple perspectives. The richness of different views from a range of involved stakeholders offers the opportunity to augment one's own 'radar' for what is and might be going wrong. The diversity here does not just cover gender, ethnicity and cultural background, but also the work background and expertise of participants. Taking on board the views of legal, commercial, finance, marketing, operations, procurement, and human resources, as well as those of technical representatives, brings in much more knowledge and insight. Every 'lookout' will be vigilant about the area he or she is familiar with and bringing them all together allows a wider sensitivity to what may go wrong or is going wrong. This does not imply, though, that multiple – often diverging – perceptions should be moulded into a single consensus view that consequently becomes anchored as a commitment. The purpose of a cross-functional perspective is to provide a rich picture, often with contradictory views, to provoke richer noticing. In this respect, it is not intended to enable simplification.

INTELLIGENT TOOLS

Most project management tools are based on the rationale of turning an uncertain environment into a single deterministic future. Instead of challenging a project manager's assumptions, they often reinforce the illusion of certainty, providing single estimates that are turned into commitments and corresponding simple 'pass/fail' criteria. Rarely is the real world this straightforward.

Any risk management system should include mechanisms to look beyond the short-term risk horizon and incorporate concepts beyond the merely more tangible criteria. It should include variables such as confidence, controllability, interdependence, and proximity to try to capture uncertainty and complexity. There are, indeed, alternatives out there to traditional risk management. A range of tools is available – among them scenario planning (see Chapter 8) – which is not designed primarily to provide an accurate prediction about a single future but to make you appreciate the variance and richness in predictions. Alertness requires tools and techniques that not only help project managers deal with the repeated past but also allow us to address uncertainty and complexity in our predictions.

LEADING THE ART OF NOTICING

Making people 'aware' in a project is a challenge and requires a leadership approach that generates honesty, transparency, and openness towards epistemic uncertainty. We do not suggest a state of paranoia in which a project is constantly thinking and 'living' failure. Such a state may only lead to exhaustion and fatalism. However, a state of 'healthy' uneasiness – a heightened and yet focussed awareness of epistemic uncertainty, is one that we can strive for. The following actions may provide a start.

BATTLING COMPLACENCY

The prolonged perception of the absence of failure, good as it might feel, is most often an indicator that people have taken their eye off the ball. At the centre of the battle against complacency is the need to make people uncomfortable by challenging them and making them less certain. Certainty about future results is comforting and pleasing, but it can be illusory. Try to play the role of 'Mr/Ms Sceptic'. Be sceptical about people's optimism that everything is going according to plan. With the help of scenarios, cultivate possible outcomes to make people think of what they should be looking out for to prevent these things from happening. Provide them with a safe culture to speak up about whatever concerns them. Even if these concerns are not tangible enough to make it on to a risk register, they are valuable pieces of information that may indicate the existence of uncertainty. In this sense, worrying is positive and valuable. First and foremost, do not try to battle complacency by turning it into a 'tick-box' exercise. Forms and documents cannot capture subtle but important information, such as emotions and gut feelings.

You may pick up signs of complacency: in meetings, people may be preoccupied with sharing their successes. Status reports may outline what has been achieved. It is the task of a leader to acknowledge and celebrate success, but also to put a question mark after every success story and to ensure time is available to raise concerns. Subtly change the way the discussion is going from what has gone right to what might still go wrong.

MOVING THE ONUS OF PROOF

Our minds like a state of 'normality'. Long periods of success may only reinforce the perception that failure will not trouble us. Managing projects can turn into a routine exercise, and, indeed, this is what most project management frameworks advocate: consistency in action as a means to reduce human situated cognition as a source of error. Under these conditions, the expectation can become one of continuing success, and it may be hard to persuade project participants of contrary possibilities. The longer this positive state of affairs continues, the more difficult it can become to raise doubts and concerns. Notions of epistemic uncertainty may be ignored or suppressed. Here, managers need to move the onus of proof. Assume that the project is inherently uncertain and complex until proven otherwise. When presented with audits and status reports that show a lot of 'green', show doubt and investigate; challenge people in their perceptions. This does not have to be confrontational but should go below the 'surface' to challenge assumptions and create greater awareness of how the project could still go off track.

Many audits in projects provide proof that everything is 'all right' (organisational incentives tend to encourage this). As a thought experiment, can you imagine an audit that provides evidence of uncertainty – about the extent of what we do not know about a future state – and complexity and yet also offers some form of evidence that the project is in a state of heightened readiness and preparedness to deal with it?

MAKING PEOPLE IMAGINE

We tend to focus on risks (aleatory uncertainty) because they are tangible and measurable and thus provide us with the comfort of (relative) certainty. But with the help of some tools, such as scenario planning, we can make people imagine beyond the risk horizon – ambiguous and difficult to measure – from a range of different perspectives. This is unlikely to provide accurate predictions about how the future will unfold, but it makes people appreciate the richness of multiple possible futures. It also gives 'permission' to worry, express doubts, and raise concerns that cannot necessarily be quantified in traditional risk management. The inability to 'prove' the existence of an issue or concern must not preclude it being brought to attention. As project leader, we can – and should – use tools that strive for accuracy and prediction. Know their limitations! Use additional techniques, not to determine a single, most likely future, but to strive to explore the murky uncertainties that normally remain undiscussed.

What we cannot measure and articulate with confidence makes us uneasy. It is preferable to stay in our comfort zones, and not worry about, let alone raise, such concerns. To reject someone's worries out of hand, or perhaps challenge them for data, sends a clear signal not to try that again. It is a delicate exercise to build greater vigilance – hard to promote, yet easy to discourage. The key is to make the team 'at ease' with feeling uneasy about uncertainty and complexity.

THE ILLUSION OF ASYMMETRIC INSIGHT

People are tribal. They may claim to celebrate the diversity of opinion and respect others' points of view but, in truth, they tend towards creating and forming groups and then believing others are wrong just because they are others. This is the essence of the illusion of asymmetric insight (Pronin et al. 2002).

This 'us and them' perspective leads to people creating views of others that are biased and partial. The source of this bias seems to stem from the unshakable belief that what we observe in others is far more revealing than our similar behaviours. It leads to stereotyping and prejudice of the 'other' and also underestimating threats from others (or, for that matter, possible partnerships and alliances).

It has been shown that we are self-deluding if we believe this and yet all human beings do this. We all hold a personal conviction that observed behaviours are more revealing of other people than of the self, while our inner voice of private thoughts and feelings are more revealing of the self. We also believe that the more we perceive negative traits of someone else, the more doubt we express about this person's self-knowledge, although we do not do this for ourselves.

This behaviour fosters conflict and misunderstanding. When others seem to see the world differently from oneself, one tends to see one's views as objective and correct, and theirs as irrational and wrong. It also means that people are irrationally closed-minded and blindly conforming – which can create serious problems in organisations that seek to be 'alive' to novelty and responsive to change (Pronin et al. 2007).

STRIPPING ADVERSITY OF ITS NEGATIVE CONNOTATIONS

The notion of risk and uncertainty as something 'bad' – although inherently natural – can be confronted by a project leader by providing different labels and connotations. Why not call risk a 'design evolution', for example? Detach the existence of uncertainty from any perception of incompetent planning, and frame its management – proactive and reactive – as an opportunity that justifies some form of reward. For example, proactive responses to uncertainty, irrespective of whether they fully work or not, should be highlighted as having prevented a worse state of affairs. Show your appreciation for the action and point out what could have happened if the measures had not been taken. The message of support for pragmatic responses is an important one. Again, if the organisational culture is one of blame and reprisal, then staff closest to the issues are unlikely to pay attention to and respond.

FOCUS ON THE ISSUE, NOT THE PERSON REPORTING IT

The negative connotations of forms of adversity may suppress the will of project members to share and report their concerns – the act of reporting might be interpreted as an acknowledgement of incompetence in preventing the failure in the first place. It is the project leader's task to focus discussion on the reported issue, not on the person reporting it. Hence, any discussion about adversity should be impersonal, although the response should have a clear owner. The focus must be on the message, not the messenger. Appreciation of where a worry or concern originates from can be useful, but the individual identifier needs to be encouraged to come forward, not incentivised to keep quiet.

ENCOURAGING THE SHARING OF ADVERSITY

It takes effort to share noticed adversity effectively. Provide your project team members with the freedom to speak up and share their perceptions. This may involve an 'open-door' policy or a standing agenda item in project meetings. Project members are then more likely to share these encounters with uncertainty with others, to allow everybody on the project to appreciate the potential problems. Often, such sharing is done by completing a form which is then reflected in an impersonal spreadsheet. Use the power of interpersonal interaction to augment this. By all means, use the necessary documentation, but build on it with more socialised sharing. People buy into stories and 'real', personal, accounts of uncertainty far more than into reading a document. Make uncertainty 'alive' to others, encourage and reward people for speaking up.

SHARED INFORMATION BIAS

Shared information bias (also known as the collective information sampling bias) is known as the tendency for group members to spend more time and energy discussing information that all members are already familiar with (e.g. shared information), and less time and energy discussing information that only some members are aware of (e.g. unshared information). Harmful consequences related to poor decision-making can arise when the group does not have access to unshared information (hidden profiles) to make a well-informed decision (Stasser and Titus 1985).

The shared information bias may also develop during a group discussion in response to the interpersonal and psychological needs of individual group members (Thompson and Wildavsky 1986). For example, some group members tend to seek group support for their own opinions. This psychological motivation to garner collective acceptance of one's initial views has been linked to group preferences for shared information during decision-making activities.

The nature of the discussion between group members reflects whether biases for shared information will surface. Members are motivated to establish and maintain reputations, to secure tighter bonds, and to compete for success against other group members. As a result, individuals tend to be selective when disclosing information to other group members.

In many ways, this kind of behaviour is counterintuitive. It seems strange that people are not eager to bring new information to group meetings to develop ideas, develop knowledge and help with decision-making. It seems that there are three main reasons why people might be reluctant to share new information (Wittenbaum et al. 2004). First, shared information is more readily recalled so is likely to be thought of first in group settings. Second, people have often decided beforehand what is important and previously shared information is what people tend to base their pre-judgments upon. Finally, and perhaps most importantly, people are often anxious about how they will be seen by other members of a group and shared information tends to take precedence. It has been found that people are regarded as being more capable when they talk about shared rather than unshared information (Wittenbaum and Bowman 2004).

In order to overcome the problems of shared information bias, consideration needs to be given to the dynamics of groups and organisational culture (Thompson and Wildavsky 1986; Wittenbaum and Bowman 2004). The foremost thing to do is to discourage groupthink. Where groups display less groupthink, they are likely to share unpooled information more readily. Additionally, expert knowledge is very important. First, if people in a group recognise the relative expertise of different group members, they are more likely to be open to new information. Second, lower status group members are more likely to be ready to speak up and contribute new information if their expertise is acknowledged by higher status group members.

THE IMPACT OF NOTICING ON RELATIONSHIPS

Noticing more, in principle, is a good thing. However, it has the potential drawback that it may confuse and unnerve your stakeholders. You may appreciate the nuances of your project and be comfortable with the discomfort of 'not knowing' with confidence, but it can be challenging to communicate this to your stakeholders.

CERTAINTY IS AN ILLUSION

Being on the lookout and noticing beyond the risk horizon, of something going or potentially going 'wrong', is a tacit acknowledgement that standard planning concepts are perhaps flawed. All the efforts that have gone into predicting the future, although valuable, are insufficient to design uncertainty out of the project completely. Uncertainty is still there, and therein lies the opportunity. Projects are often sold on the premise of certainty, so stakeholders can sit back and see a plan turn into reality. Stakeholders such as sponsors need to understand that epistemic uncertainty is 'normal' and that, despite all the efforts that go into planning, estimates remain estimates, or are mere speculations. Many aspects remain unknown. Without such an acknowledgement, there is limited need for vigilance and desire to look beyond what has been planned for.

MINDFUL PRACTICES

This vignette on shortening the planning horizon looks at arguably one of the most hotly debated and contested aspects of project management. A range of organisations shorten their planning horizons under the umbrella of 'Agile' project management. However, we wish to highlight that this approach could and should be applied in projects characterised by uncertainty, regardless of whether the fundamental approach to managing uncertainty is a (mini-)waterfall approach, or interactive and incremental.

ITERATIONS

At Intel, projects are predominantly run by following the agile philosophy. Part of that philosophy is the definition of iterations. Iterations are single planning and development cycles, ranging from two to six weeks. These cycles are of fixed lengths within a project but can vary across projects:

In the past you probably would have had to have gone down the route of explaining to them [stakeholders] that we had six-monthly planning and design cycles and so we'd get to it when we do, it's brilliant now to be able to say to them, OK, well we'll take the requirement, we've got a planning session coming up in to say three weeks' time, we'll look at it against all of the other priorities that we've got but hopefully, we can get that scheduled and then within seven weeks from now you'll be able to get that new piece of functionality scheduled and it is something that

*our business stakeholders are really appreciating, and it just
helps to build that partnership with our stakeholders ...*

At the end of an iteration, there may be the release of output,
the achievement of a milestone, or a design review. However,
it is not the output of an iteration that defines its length as
duration is fixed for repeatability. Releases to the customer can
be made at the end of one or many iterations or more frequently
in alignment with customers' needs. After the completion of an
iteration, it is reviewed and critiqued by stakeholders – such
as the end-user – to accommodate flexibility in revising the
ultimate goal to be achieved and the way to get there. This form
of instrumentalism allows managers to plan an iteration based on
learning gained from the previous one:

> *You need some certain expectations at the start of a project
> that the customer has availability and time so they can provide
> enough input into the project to make sure that we're able to
> keep the team moving forward at the optimal velocity because if
> you don't get the feedback then the team kind of stalls ...*

The benefits of having such incremental iterations in place are
numerous:

- Transparency and visibility: stakeholders receive insight and
  give feedback not just at the end of a project but throughout.
- Flexibility: frequent reviews and critiques allow timely
  changes in what to do next and where to go.
- Collaboration: iterations 'enforce' frequent interactions between
  stakeholders and the provider, with influence from both sides
  on changing ways of working and the goals to be achieved.

The enablers to achieving such visibility, flexibility and
collaboration are based on setting expectations. Parties involved
need to accept project autonomy, with everyone having their say.
That autonomy is built on trust. Iterations are not purposeful if
they are only used as a means of checking what another party

does. Instead, beyond providing transparency and thus visibility, they offer a platform to experience progress in delivering a solution while having the comfort of flexibility to change it:

> *you maybe don't want your customer involved in every single one of them [iteration] but ultimately they will probably affect your output and so having the trust of your customer who in turn then gives you the autonomy to make those decisions on their behalf is an important aspect of it.*

Another form of using iterative planning is 'Rolling Wave' planning. This is a process whereby you plan part of the project while the work is being delivered. As the project proceeds and its latter stages become clearer, additional planning can take place. At the outset, high-level assumptions are made and broad milestones set which become more concrete as the project progresses. As activities are undertaken, assumptions become better defined, and milestones become more precise.

At TTP, it is often the case that the client is unsure of exactly what they need to do to solve their problem. Indeed, they may be unsure of the true nature of the problem itself. TTP's project leaders must be able to adapt their planning:

> *on say a year's program we have at least three phases in there ... concept phase, detailed design phase and then the transfer to production phase so that at the end of each phase, then you can both assess. We can assess, and the client can assess – did we achieve the goals? Were we on a budget? Is the product within the specification? And all those sorts of things, and so the more phases we have in, the better, in some respects, because you're checking it.*

Each phase constitutes, in principle, a new contract, yet with shortened planning horizons to allow greater flexibility in adjusting each phase in the light of new information. Rolling wave planning at TTP takes uncertainty into account and provides the benefit of not having to 'fix' the entirety of the project.

Functional circumstances frequently constrain the duration of a phase. As it is applied in TTP, phases are often defined by their functions of concept, design, and production. Alternatively, phases can be demarcated by a certain level of confidence. The only 'fixed' durations are for those phases for which project managers are sufficiently confident. If estimates are deemed unreliable, the planning horizon will be shortened accordingly. Uncertainty in estimating – characterised by the level of confidence – plays an important role in determining how long a 'wave' may be.

Whether they are called rolling wave or incremental, iterative planning, these concepts have one thing in common – shortening the planning horizon to accommodate uncertainty. The flexibility in goals, approach and our interpretation of these aspects – it is all in the eye of the beholder – requires constant collaboration with all stakeholders involved.

At Aviva, similar to what is being prescribed in major agile project management standards, interactions between stakeholders are facilitated in the form of 'Scrum' meetings, to open a discussion on how they could potentially do something differently:

> *If someone has a new idea they can feed that back into the scrum so they could say, 'you've asked us to do this to get this result but actually if we did that, you get a better result', and then the project manager would take that back to the business to make sure the new proposal works for them.*

Participants at these meetings are all major stakeholders. The meetings do not tend to last longer than 15 minutes, to keep the discussion focussed on relevant reflection and corrections, and also to address the overall project goal and approach.

> *We have a daily 15 minutes scrum meeting, and everybody that has an interest in this can attend that meeting, including any third party resources that we're using.*

For the sake of emphasis, three questions are addressed:

- What did you do yesterday?
- What will you do today?
- Are there any impediments in your way?

These questions may sound mundane and, if repeatedly asked, stakeholders might find them distracting and irrelevant. However, the purpose is to ensure the ongoing transparency of what is going on with all the stakeholders together. Issues and blockages can then be quickly resolved, allowing the project to move on.

Traditional project management may entail monthly planning cycles and weekly interactions. However, all our organisations – Intel, TTP, and Aviva – appreciate the need to shorten the planning horizon in their projects; to have short iterations and daily updates.

What is mindful about it? Venturing beyond the risk horizon requires an iterative process of planning. It is a continuous process of challenging mindsets of what is 'not known', perceiving and re-perceiving what epistemic uncertainty entails, and whether our actions match the present situation or a plan that is already 'out of date'.

Referring to the methodology of Agile Project Management, a planning cycle tends to be 30 days to six weeks. It is consistent with the degree of foresight individuals can make sense of and confidently cope with.

REPORTING BEYOND BOUNDARIES

One might assume that the project team does all the noticing. But why not enlarge your 'radar' beyond your internal boundaries? Use the wider group of stakeholders as lookouts who are vigilant enough constantly, or at least repeatedly, to raise their concerns with you. Their interests and yours should be aligned with regards to everyone's desire to see the project succeed. If possible, initiate this right at the start of the project, to involve them imagining beyond a short-term risk horizon. This can create a shared understanding of the project environment and how best to handle it. Without their engagement as part of project radar, they may interpret any unplanned change as a surprise.

You have a choice in addressing uncertainty. You can choose to 'sell' your project by showing (off) your planning and portraying the project as certain. In this case, there may be a limited need to be on the lookout for epistemic uncertainty, difficult as it may be to do so anyway. However, you also have the opportunity to use your stakeholders' capability to be on the lookout, and consequently to integrate them into your noticing radar. Hence, in meetings with them, feel free to ask about their opinions and gut instincts. Be reluctant to focus solely on what has gone well in a project; drive the discussion about the future, beyond the risk horizon. It is always worthwhile asking 'What do you think might go wrong?'

CONSISTENCY IN RELATIONSHIPS

The ability to notice and share beyond boundaries forms the pillars of an 'informed' culture, in which all parties understand each other's perspectives, even if they are mutually contradictory. This implies that if stakeholders understand your perspectives, they are more capable of looking out for you and noticing on your behalf. It is less a notion of 'I know better' than a way of adding to the richness of the overall project knowledge and understanding. It requires, however, that you guide your stakeholders to an understanding of your position, and vice versa. Vigilance can only be instilled if parties learn to understand each other's stances through communication, transparency and trust.

PAYING FOR SUPPOSEDLY IDLE RESOURCES

To be vigilant, to notice beyond the measurable and tangible, one needs 'space' in the form of time and resources to look out, to challenge others in their complacency, to encourage and motivate people to do it themselves and actively share their perceptions, perhaps even to think and reflect. Such activities do not necessarily directly contribute to the execution of the project; they help you to prepare and ready yourself for something that may never materialise. Hence, the resourcing of such activities is by no means uncontroversial (especially for budget-holders). A heightened state of awareness comes at a price, without necessarily producing tangible and measurable outcomes. Stakeholders require a shared understanding that noticing more is an art for which faith in its success replaces proof.

KODAK – A FAILURE OF NOTICING

In January 2012, Kodak, an American technology company that concentrated on imaging products and had invented the hand-held camera, filed for bankruptcy. What was once considered a hub of technological wizardry suddenly became an institution with little hope of surviving much longer into the future.

The demise of Kodak, like nothing else, highlights the ongoing need for top-level managers to cope with the effects of uncertainty. The use of photographic film was pioneered by George Eastman, who started manufacturing paper film in 1885 before switching to celluloid in 1889. His first camera, which he called the 'Kodak', was first offered for sale in 1888. It was a very simple box camera with a fixed-focus lens and single shutter speed which, along with its relatively low price appealed to the average consumer. The first camera using digital electronics to capture and store images was developed by 1975. The adoption of digital cameras was slow. In 1999, with the rise of broadband technology to share digital images, the demand for stand-alone digital cameras exploded, fuelled by the introduction of the iPhone in 2007. The volatility in the environment, amplified by the rise of the smartphone, caught Kodak off guard, partially because of its lack of understanding of market volatility.

Epistemic uncertainty is associated with a lack of predictability about how the environment will unfold, and the lack of awareness and understanding of developments, issues and events:

Kodak's top management never fully grasped how the world around them was changing. They hung on to now obsolete assumptions about who took pictures, why and when.

(Munir 2016)

Recent generations of Kodak manager were too wedded to the past business model to take the radical steps needed to reposition their company as a digital leader. In other words, they were too comfortable about their business model, assuming however the environment will change around Kodak, their 'proven' ways of working will weather any storm. Kodak, as an organisation, became too comfortable in believing in their invincibility.

To notice more, organisations need to create organisational instruments of discomfort, such as those described in this chapter. People in an organisation need to be able to speak up about potential failure, they need to imagine beyond the risk horizon before the competitions impose its will on the organisation. The potential to fail as an organisation needs to be brought to the forefront, so the organisational mind creates a capability to notice more warning signals of change and impending failure.

TOWARDS AN ART OF NOTICING

The art of noticing is built on the need to look beyond the risk horizon, beyond what we expect to be 'normal', and beyond established organisational boundaries. The benefit is not necessarily to increase the accuracy of prediction, but – to put it simply – to keep on noticing more and become increasingly aware of issues beyond the measurable and familiar, beyond aleatory uncertainty. Such a heightened state of awareness towards epistemic uncertainty is characterised by a healthy uneasiness (although without switching to a state of paranoia) about the unknown and unexpected. Such a project is one in which participants keep their eyes on what is or might be going wrong instead of blindly focusing on what has gone right or is expected to go right.

Reflection

How well do the following statements characterise your project? For each item, select one box only that best reflects your conclusion.

	Fully disagree		Neither agree nor disagree		Fully agree
We acknowledge that our initial estimates are just that, estimates.	1	2	3	4	5
We communicate uncertainty in our planning.	1	2	3	4	5
People are provided with 'space' (e.g. time) to look out for things that could go wrong.	1	2	3	4	5

	Fully disagree		Neither agree nor disagree		Fully agree
We aim to increase the perceived uncertainty of project participants.	1	2	3	4	5
People are constructively challenged in their estimates.	1	2	3	4	5
We make people think about the uncertainties that cannot be specified.	1	2	3	4	5

	Fully disagree		Neither agree nor disagree		Fully agree
We use intelligent tools and techniques that not only take into account what we know but also what we do not know.	1	2	3	4	5
People are encouraged to share risks and uncertainties beyond their set boundaries.	1	2	3	4	5
Risk and uncertainty are seen as something 'good' to look out for.	1	2	3	4	5

Scoring: Add the numbers. If you score higher than 27, your capability to be more discriminatory in your noticing of uncertainty is good. If you score 27 or lower, please think of how you can expand and enhance your capability of noticing uncertainty beyond the risk horizon.

REFERENCES

Christensen-Szalanski, J. J. J., and L. Roy Beach. 2006. "The Citation Bias: Fad and Fashion in the Judgment and Decision Literature." *American Psychologist* 39(1): 75–78.

Denrell, J. 2003. "Vicarious Learning, Undersampling of Failure, and the Myths of Management." *Organization Science* 14(3): 227–43.

Denrell, J. 2005. "Selection Bias and the Perils of Benchmarking – Harvard Business Review." *Harward Business Review* 83(4): 114–19.

Ellenberg, J. 2015. *How Not to Be Wrong: The Hidden Maths of Everyday Life.* London: Penguin Books.

Haith, A. M., T. R. Reppert, and R. Shadmehr. 2012. "Evidence for Hyperbolic Temporal Discounting of Reward in Control of Movements." *Journal of Neuroscience* 32(34): 11727–36.

Munir, K. 2016. "The Demise of Kodak: Five Reasons." *Wall Street Journal.* http://blogs.wsj.com/source/2012/02/26/the-demise-of-kodak-five-reasons/.

Omer, H., and N. Alon. 1994. "The Continuity Principle: A Unified Approach to Disaster and Trauma." *American Journal of Community Psychology* 22(2): 273–87.

Perry, R. W., M. K. Lindell, and M. R. Greene. 1982. "Threat Perception and Public Response to Volcano Hazard." *Journal of Social Psychology* 116(2): 199–204.

Pronin, E., J. Berger, and S. Molouki. 2007. "Alone in a Crowd of Sheep: Asymmetric Perceptions of Conformity and Their Roots in an Introspection Illusion." *Journal of Personality and Social Psychology* 92(4): 585–95.

Pronin, E., D. Y. Lin, and L. Ross. 2002. "The Bias Blind Spot: Perceptions of Bias in Self versus Others." *Personality and Social Psychology Bulletin* 28(3): 369–81.

Roese, N. J., and K. D. Vohs. 2012. "Hindsight Bias." *Perspectives on Psychological Science* 7(5): 411–26.

Stasser, G., and W. Titus. 1985. "Pooling of Unshared Information in Group Decision Making: Biased Information Sampling during Discussion." *Journal of Personality and Social Psychology* 48(6): 1467–78.

Thompson, M., and A. Wildavsky. 1986. "A Cultural Theory of Information Bias in Organizations." *Journal of Management Studies* 23(3): 273–86.

Wittenbaum, G. M., and J. M. Bowman. 2004. "A Social Validation Explanation for Mutual Enhancement." *Journal of Experimental Social Psychology* 40(2): 169–84.

Wittenbaum, G. M., A. B. Hollingshead, and I. C. Botero. 2004. "From Cooperative to Motivated Information Sharing in Groups: Moving beyond the Hidden Profile Paradigm." *Communication Monographs* 71(3): 286–310.

CHAPTER FOUR

The art of interpreting

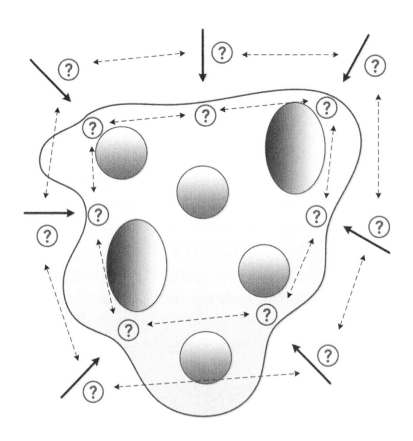

CONTENTS

Project uncertainty is in the eye of the beholder. It's an interpretation of what we do and do not think we know. It is based on interpretations and judgement, a product of social interaction, a continuous construction and reconstruction. In a project, we continually seek to make sense of what is going on, and the nuance of this process of making sense of the world is crucial to the management of uncertainty.

At the beginning of any uncertain endeavour, stakeholders will probably demand certainty. In other words, the question of 'What will it all mean?' is central to the discussion at a point when stakeholders long for the comfort of having confidence in a simple, predictable, controllable future.

THE LURE OF SIMPLICITY

In order to cope with uncertainty, we tend to simplify, so that we can move on. We filter out cues in the environment that prohibits forthright action. The process of simplification is inherently detrimental to the management of uncertainty. It reinforces complacency and ignorance of the attendant uncertainty. Processes of simplification may do little more than result in an *illusion* of control.

STRUCTURAL OVERSIMPLIFICATION

A project is often understood in terms of its constituent elements, for example, using a work breakdown structure. This produces a seemingly (relatively) simple set of tasks and activities, and there is a corresponding tendency for the project team to regard the project as being reasonably straightforward.

Because we tend to look at aspects of adversity in isolation, we often tend to pay little heed to the 'big picture'. Aristotle's famous 'The whole is greater than the sum of its parts' is valid in projects, too. By applying traditional planning tools, we can emphasise our tendency to oversimplify and thus underestimate uncertainty and complexity. This uncertainty and complexity is not just related to the specific activities, but also their inter-relationship as a project system and the project's connection to other, related projects and the wider supply network and stakeholder community. Projects are all about inter-relationships and interdependencies and failure to understand this is to seriously underestimate inherent epistemic uncertainty.

OPTIMISM BIAS

First described by Weinstein (1980) in the 1980s, irrational optimism bias is perhaps the best known among the many cognitive biases under which all people labour. For many decades, scientists have recognised that people tend to underestimate their chances of negative experiences while overestimating their chances of positive experiences (Shah et al. 2016). Optimism bias – sometimes called the 'illusion of invulnerability' or 'unrealistic optimism' – has, at its heart, a natural inclination among people to exceptionalism. This means that we have regard of ourselves that is greater than that of people in general, a perspective that gives rise to the term the 'personal fable', describing the view we hold about ourselves as the protagonist in our own life story. The consequences can be profound. It manifests itself in personal beliefs we hold about ourselves and our immediate family such as that we will live longer than the average, that our children will be smarter than the norm and that we will be more successful in life than the average. By definition, however, we cannot all be above average.

The point about optimism bias is that our tendency to overestimate outcomes of our actions means that people make poor decisions (Sharot 2016). In our personal lives, people take unnecessary risks as they feel they will not suffer detrimental consequences. For example, people might choose not to wear seatbelts, or to use their mobile phone while driving. Here, they are overestimating their driving skills. Similarly, we might not see the doctor when we need to because we overestimate our health.

That said, optimism bias is not always problematic. The benefits of optimism bias are that we are more likely to pursue our goals and take risks required to achieve objectives. Without optimism bias, some things would never be attempted. This gives rise to a conundrum. If people overestimate their chances of success in the things they do because of optimism bias, they are likely to make poor, mindless decisions. However, optimism bias is essential so that people attempt any undertakings they might otherwise reject as being too risky (Sharot 2016).

What applies to our personal lives also plays out in organisational life (Kahneman and Lovallo 2003). The same poor decision-making in our everyday lives can easily translate into poor decisions in business investments or government spending. In a study, 11,600 Chief Financial Officer (CFO) forecasts were compared against market outcomes, and a correlation was found of less than zero. This shows that CFOs are grossly over-confident about their ability to forecast the market (Kahneman and Lovallo 2003). While optimism is vital to having persistence in the face of obstacles, pervasive optimism bias can be detrimental. For example, only 35 per cent of small businesses survive in the US. When surveyed, however, 81 per cent of entrepreneurs assessed their odds of success at 70 per cent, and 33 per cent of them went so far as to put their chances at 100 per cent.

While this may not be such a problem in smaller-scale organisations, when it involves significant capital investments, optimism bias of this nature can be disastrous for organisations. It results in capital being invested in projects that never had a chance of receiving a return, or of excessive tax income being invested in projects that have small benefits. More importantly, when things start to go wrong, people in organisations have a tendency to overestimate their ability to get projects back on track, which means they pursue objectives with no realistic chance of achieving them, even when this becomes apparent.

A good example was the dramatic rise and sudden downfall of Theranos. The company was set up to develop technology to carry out a barrage of blood tests quickly and simply from just a few drops of blood. The benefits in terms of savings both of blood test costs and lives through quick results were tantalising but the CEO, Elizabeth Holmes, grossly overestimated the ability of her company to successfully develop the technology required while large American firms and famous investors such as Walgreens and Safeway invested hundreds of millions of dollars into an unproven technology, over-optimistic of its promise and the abilities of the team at Theranos to deliver it (Carreyrou 2018).

Optimism bias is more likely to occur where events are infrequent, such as one-off projects. People are also more likely to experience optimism bias where they think they have direct control or influence over events. This is not because they believe that things will necessarily go well in some fateful way, but that they overestimate their skills and capabilities to control things. Finally, optimism bias is likely to occur where the negative consequences of an undertaking are perceived to be unlikely, even if this perception is misplaced. By contrast, experiencing certain events for real can reduce optimism and people, it has been found, are less likely to be over-optimistic when comparing themselves to very close friends, family and colleagues (Sharot 2016).

As can be seen, optimism bias has benefits and problems. It is necessary to be optimistic to motivate employees and keep them focused, and optimism encourages people in organisations to take challenges and not be overly risk-averse. However, optimism bias tends to be more about enthusiasm than realism (Kahneman and Lovallo 2003) and, therefore, organisations have to find a way of maintaining a balance between over-optimism and realism. For organisations, perhaps the most important thing to do is to draw a clear distinction between the individuals, where optimism encourages vision and innovation, and functions tasked with supporting decision-making, where mindful realism should prevail (Kahneman and Lovallo 2003).

'NO EFFECT ON ME'

Going hand-in-hand with optimism bias is the belief among many that adversity will not affect our project. We have planned it meticulously and carried out a detailed risk planning and management process. Just as no one on their wedding day believes that their marriage will end in divorce, so too do we tend to think that our project is invulnerable or, perhaps, impervious to adversity. We do not believe this is without agency – we feel that there is something special about us and what we do that will avert problems, either as individuals or as a collective. The result is that we are likely to focus on 'doing the job' (e.g. working on project tasks) rather than looking for those early, weak signals of uncertainty. Adversity may hit other projects, but it will not happen in this – our – project.

THE REALM OF PROBABILITY AND IMPACT

The process of risk management is driven by a relatively simple principle – the likelihood of an event occurring and the probable impact should that event occur. This straightforward approach (likelihood × severity) underpins nearly all standard risk assessments. The orthodox approach is to focus on those risks with a high combination of the two and ignore, or downplay, those with a low probability of occurrence or a little impact should they occur, or both. This can be problematic, as traditional risk assessments do not tend to capture what we do not know, or in other words, what risks we are not confident about. It is a striking feature of typical risk management process in project management that the extent of epistemic uncertainty is not advocated to be measured.

ESTIMATES BECOME COMMITMENTS

The future is difficult to predict accurately and to explain, but at the beginning of projects, this is precisely what we are asked to do. We are required to forecast the duration and cost of a project, frequently in the face of intense uncertainty. The estimate we arrive at is essentially the process of putting a value against that uncertainty, governed by a combination of experience and the information available at the time. Owing to the subjective nature of estimating, it can be an inherently personal, human-made, fact-based fiction that we tell ourselves about the time and resource commitment necessary to complete a task. This is a function of not only the project's inherent difficulties, but also our capacity to combat them. Perhaps the fundamental problem with estimating projects is that the estimate is based on an idealised conception of productivity – an idealisation often based on optimism. The real problem happens when the project team and sponsors equate the estimate with a firm commitment. This can have an unwanted effect on behaviours (such as Anchoring). Organisations that demand adherence to original estimates unwittingly promote 'padding' in the next set of estimates to increase the likelihood of meeting them. Too much padding – although a perfectly rational response from each individual's perspective – makes the estimate uncompetitive and may lead to the loss of a bid or the work not even being funded.

When estimates have become commitments, these commitments serve as anchors for subsequent decisions about what resources to commit to the project. The tendency to do this is due to over-optimism about the reliability of the estimate. Because of the optimism bias that was built into the original figures, any subsequent analysis is also skewed to over-optimism. Data disconfirming those estimates are discounted, and those reinforcing the estimates are amplified. The results are exaggerated benefits, unrealistic costs, and an almost inevitable project disappointment.

ANCHORING

Another cognitive bias that has long been recognised (Tversky and Kahneman 1974), and can be found both in peoples' everyday lives and in business, is anchoring bias, sometimes referred to as focalism. It occurs when people over-rely either on information they already possess or on the first information they find when making decisions. In an often-quoted example, if someone sees a shirt priced at $1,000 and a second priced at $100, they might view the other shirt as being cheap, whereas if they had only seen the $100 shirt, they would probably not view it as a bargain. The first shirt in this example is the anchor, unduly influencing the opinion of the value of the second shirt. That said, it has been found that anchoring only occurs typically where the anchor information is not ridiculous (Sugden et al. 2013). However, if the anchor figure is not perceived as being ridiculous, even arbitrary numbers can be found to act as an anchor.

Anchoring can happen in all sorts of aspects of daily life. For example, if both parents of someone live a long life, that person might also expect to live a long life, perhaps ignoring that their parents had healthier and more active lifestyles than they do. If a person watched a lot of television as a child, they might think it is acceptable for their children to do the same. In healthcare, a physician might inaccurately diagnose a patient's illness as their first impressions of the patient's symptoms can create an anchor point that impacts all subsequent assessments. These are all examples of anchoring, where people make estimates by starting from an initial value that is adjusted to yield the final answer (Tversky and Kahneman 1974).

Marketing departments have long recognised the power of anchoring to influence customer purchasing decisions. For example, a retailer may purposely inflate the price of an item for a short period so that they can show a substantial discount. The inflated cost acts as the anchor making the product seem relatively cheap (Levine 2006).

In organisations, anchoring can frequently be seen at play (Daniel Kahneman and Lovallo 2003). Where organisations are making investment decisions, anchoring is particularly pernicious. A team might draw up plans and proposals for an investment based on market research, financial analysis, or their professional judgment before arriving at decisions about whether and how to proceed. On the face of it, this is uncontroversial, but all the analysis tends to be overly optimistic and is often anchored to whatever the initial budget or estimate happened to be (Kutsch et al. 2011). It can go as far as whole teams of stakeholders developing a delusion that their accurate assessments are entirely objective when, in fact, they were anchored all along (Flyvjberg 2005).

AMNESIA

We often try to put difficult or trying times behind us by simply forgetting about them – 'out of sight, out of mind'. Attention moves on to something else (for example, a new project) and we frequently stop thinking about the difficulties we previously faced. This can happen simply because we do not want to think about troubling times, or because some project members move on (retire, move to new organisations) and knowledge is dissipated. Having to tackle emerging uncertainty is painful, uncomfortable for us. It is no surprise that we will forget about them over time. It is a well-established phenomenon within the literature that organisations struggle to learn from previous projects.

THE PERCEPTION OF LOSSES AND GAINS

We tend to interpret potential gains and losses differently. Facing a loss triggers stronger stimuli to respond than facing a gain or an opportunity. In a project, a potential loss may thus receive more attention than is given to a possibly more valuable opportunity. Once materialised, actual losses may be a focus for attention while more beneficial opportunities remain under- or unexploited. This response system can create a spiralling effect, where we stubbornly try to make up for lost ground, missing alternative options that would, when viewed objectively, offer more advantageous uses of time and resources.

LOSS AVERSION

For many people, losses loom larger than gains. As a result, people try to avoid losing things more than they seek to gain things of equivalent value (Kahneman and Tversky 1991). Having to give up objects makes people anxious and, ironically, the more people have, the more anxious they feel at a possible loss. Psychologists have found that the pain of losing something is almost twice as powerful an emotion as the pleasure of gaining something (Rick 2011) and explains why people are more likely to take greater risks (and even behave dishonestly) in order to avoid losses (Schindler and Pfattheicher 2017). This manifests itself in everyday life, for example, feeling blame more acutely than praise. There is a central paradox to loss aversion. People tend to be risk-averse when faced with the possibility of losses and, at the same time, are prepared to take risks to avoid those same losses.

Loss aversion bias can manifest itself in a number of ways in organisations. The three most common are:

1. The endowment effect, where people are reluctant to invest in new capital because they overvalue what they already have, regardless of its objective market value, and forgetting that things depreciate (Kahneman and Tversky 1991).
2. The sunk cost fallacy, where people continue with a plan or endeavour despite getting no gain from it because of the time, effort and resources already committed to the endeavour (Arkes and Blumer 1985).
3. The status quo bias or conformity, where people stick with earlier decisions rather than drop them for new courses of action. This is a significant problem for organisations seeking to implement change as it breeds inertia and closes people off to opportunities and solutions (Ryan 2016).

OVERANALYSING

The opposite pole to oversimplification is overanalysing. We may be tempted to devise the 'perfect' plan that is very detailed and provides a supposedly accurate picture of how the project will unfold. Analysing in too much detail may strip us from paying attention to what the plan does not tell us, of how much we do not yet know.

The danger is that we end up ricocheting from one extreme to another; from oversimplification as a means to move on to overanalysing to provide us and our stakeholders with details and an illusion of certainty. Both extremes are detrimental to our ability to deal with epistemic uncertainty.

KEY ENABLERS TO THE ART OF INTERPRETING

Our interpretation of uncertainty and complexity is clouded by cognitive biases, preventing us from think mindfully about the future. What can we do about it?

BIG PICTURE THINKING

To find the right balance between oversimplifying and overanalysing the future of a project, big picture thinking is essential. Looking at the big picture involves trying to see the entire scope of a task or a project, as an entity, a system and a network of systems. This can be a tactical way to obtain a full sense or understanding of things.

So, what are these big strategic questions that we may not be spending enough time on or are not answering in a sufficiently clear or disciplined way? They are questions about:

- why the project exists and what its purpose is;
- what it offers (and does not offer) its stakeholders, and how and why this these offers deliver value to customers,;
- what this produces for the stakeholders – the critical outcome metrics by which the project will be judged;
- and how the people within the project will behave – toward stakeholders, and each other.

DEVIL'S ADVOCATE

There is a misconception about seeking consensus and direction in decision-making through people's engagement in dialogue. This is generally not the best approach if decisions need to be made not only quickly but also effectively. Dialogue involves conversations between people with mutual concerns but no task-orientation or any necessity to persuade others to accept a position. What is more useful in decision-making, where task and direction are essential, is dialectics.

Dialectics privilege rationality in an argument to arrive at a consensual 'truth'. The role of the 'devil's advocate' is influential in arguing against that dominant position of a simplistic future. That role is to resist and to point out flaws in deeply embedded simplification of a future state a project. The devil's advocate increases both the number and quality of decision-making alternatives and can be a catalyst for new ideas. Devil's advocacy can be used both in early decision-making stages and also as a post-decision critique. It usually is best undertaken by someone separate from the group: an outsider who is both structurally and emotionally detached from the project or problem being considered.

MINDFUL PRACTICES

RISK INTERDEPENDENCIES

At Aviva, the issue of interdependencies between risks is actively addressed. In doing so, Aviva is seeking to acknowledge that one risk may influence other risks, not only within the boundaries of a single project but, possibly, also across project and organisational boundaries. A range of tools is utilised to encourage project leaders to think about risk interdependencies. One tool that can easily be applied to address risk complexity is causal mapping. Causal mapping has its origin in strategic management but can be used in any context that involves some complexity. At Aviva, this consists of visualising interdependencies, which are then mapped, often in the form of a cognitive map or mind map (see Figure 4.1).

In this example, particular attention has to be paid to Risk D, as it influences other risks beyond the project boundary.

There is no single right answer as to how to develop these causal maps. Elements can be coloured differently, for example, to highlight risks that affect critical components in one or more projects. A key objective of such maps, however, is to trigger an

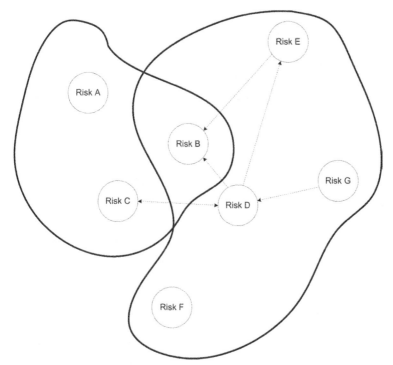

Figure 4.1 *Example of a causal map*

exploration of problems – risks in this example – but also solutions. As much as risks can interact with each other, so can solutions.

Aviva sees both uncertainty and complexity as issues to be addressed through understanding the interrelationships and seeking practical solutions. To some, it may seem a futile exercise to move beyond the isolationist management of risk to explore risk and response interdependencies. For others, it is a revelation that provides another step in appreciating complexity in modern-day project management.

What is mindful about it? Perhaps first and foremost, we should be helped to understand the interdependencies between different parts of the project, between the project and the wider environment and between the various stakeholders. There are several strategies that can be used to help us think in terms of connections and relationships. For example, liberal use of 'rich pictures' associated with soft systems methodology (SSM), can help people understand the interconnectedness of project systems. SSM focuses on seeing project systems as mental models of interconnection and is a way of revealing and understanding different world-views. Understanding connections between elements of a system and across different systems is the first step in avoiding oversimplification and over-optimism. It illustrates, in a very vivid manner, the complexities of a project and the scope for uncertainty to emerge.

MEMORY

For projects, organisational amnesia means that past risks, and their causes can easily be forgotten. A way of tackling this phenomenon is to refresh the memory and surface previous, possibly unpleasant or painful, experiences. Although a wide range of IT-based codification systems has been developed, it is crucial to recognise the importance of relationship-based memory within the organisation. Although it is widely studied in the academic literature, the value of social interaction is often underplayed within practitioner-focused work. 'Social capital' (which is comparable to financial or human capital) is often vital in 'getting things done', and most managers intuitively recognise this. Because it is a somewhat intangible concept and hard to quantify, though, we are generally reluctant to try and 'manage' it. However, strong relationships build trust and a network of trusted colleagues built over time is hugely valuable. Speaking to someone and using their knowledge often also seems more 'real' and relevant, and even more trustworthy, than reading documents in a lessons-learnt database. In a team-based environment, members also soon learn 'who-knows-what', and this, in turn, leads to efficiency in knowledge-sharing and knowledge generation that surpasses what would be the case in a newly-formed team.

To encourage these activities, some practical things we can do are to put in place mechanisms for reflecting and learning from experience; to focus feedback from peers or managers on experiential learning and to support learning both within the team and from outside the team through the sharing of experiences. Some mechanisms that can be put in place to support this kind of learning and prompting of memories are communities of practice and the use of storytelling techniques. The latter are often rich and provoking and constitute an effective way of learning and fixing experiences in mind.

MINDFUL PRACTICES

MAINTAINING AND RETAINING KNOWLEDGE

While working on a project, it is important to understand what the significant knowledge is (the 'how' of the work), and who the best people are to go to for expertise and advice. Ensuring that this is effective, and that staff can learn from such experts, is a key part of practical knowledge management. As one project manager told us:

> We try and keep knowledge experts in their positions so they
> can help kind of coach and bring up other people within
> the team, certainly in some of the projects that we've been
> involved in where we have almost a core nucleus of permanent
> employees who are working on a particular project and have
> done in that particular area for quite some time, you find that
> the benefits really start to get shared across the team because,
> if you've got on the periphery of the project, people that are
> maybe coming and going or aren't around for so long, can really
> learn and be coached by those other people.

At Intel, despite the inherent uncertainty in the problems, solutions and stakeholders they are engaged with, they try to maintain pools of project teams so that knowledge and capabilities are as stable as possible. They will add understanding if required.

Technical expertise, as well as familiarity, are brought together and maintained.

This 'pooling' of knowledge, however, does not guarantee a commitment to retain it over time. With increasing experience, valuable knowledge workers may be promoted away from where their insight is most useful. Promotion of skilled and knowledgeable staff can deprive projects of expertise. To deal with this problem, Intel developed a culture that encourages experts to remain close and committed to the project at hand. As we were told:

> It's one of the very strong corporation cultures that we have in terms of making sure that your career develops well. Intel is an organisation that doesn't allow people to get into a 'comfy seat'. We encourage you to push you on continually. Our internal structures allow that, so at every stage, they then push you on, and you get a greater level of responsibility. Thus, in our project, where we have this core nucleus who have probably been in that kind of role for a while, we start to ask them to start coaching, mentoring the more junior, less experienced, members of the team so that they are almost creating their own succession plan. Then, when it does get to that point where they've reached the level to move up, you've then built up some people behind them that can take over from them.

What is mindful about it? To retain knowledge, one could offer a monetary incentive. That is not necessarily the best route, though, since if we are paid more for our specific expertise, we have a strong disincentive to share what we know. This can reward entirely the wrong behaviours. Looking more broadly, knowledge experts:

- tend to be specialised, yet have an interest in looking beyond their specialism. Employers may offer insights and challenges from different perspectives.

- tend to believe in independency and often do not like to be 'boxed in' by hierarchy. It is not the hierarchical position that defines a knowledge expert but the value they can offer. The meaning in their work is not limited by status per se but by the development of knowledge that can be accessed for the good of the project. The respect of peers is a strong motivator.

- tend to be lifelong learners. They constantly need to maintain their interest by being challenged and pushing their boundaries. Allowing them to do this and offering them these opportunities keeps them interested, and thus committed and more likely to stay within a project team.

VALUE-DRIVEN PROJECT MANAGEMENT

The reason projects are undertaken is to deliver value for the organisation (whether private-, public- or third-sector). This may involve specific products or services and can even encompass safety and regulatory compliance projects. Given (broadly) that business or taxpayer value is the reason for doing projects, it makes sense that there is a focus on value-driven delivery. The concept of risk is closely associated with value, so much so that sometimes we think of risk as 'anti–value'. This is because, if they occur, risks have the potential to erode value. The notion of value is also closely tied to differing definitions of success, with project delivery criteria in terms of budget and time frequently overlapping only briefly with the actual business needs of the sponsoring organisation. So, following a project plan to conclusion may not lead to success if value-adding changes are not implemented effectively.

The purpose of value-driven project management is to shift the focus from the detailed delivery of project activities to understanding what value means for a customer and end-user stakeholders and, in doing so, concentrating on what matters in the project. If the project team is concentrating on this value, then their focus is what 'matters'.

There are some techniques associated with this kind of value approach that can be employed. Many have the added advantage of emphasising the creative potential of the project team. Techniques that might be applied to enhance project value include:

- Functional Analysis (sometimes called the 'functional analysis systems technique' – FAST). This is a method of analysis that can be applied to the individual functional parts of a project, identifying and emphasising the intended outcomes of the project as opposed to outputs or methods of delivery. Each aspect can be described with a 'verb-noun – phrase or adjective' combination, which focuses the thinking.
- Life-cycle costing and whole-life value techniques. Here, the focus is on how costs are incurred and value derived from the outputs of a project right through its useful life. Costs that might be considered include the original development costs, plus the deployment costs over its lifetime (the total running costs including maintenance and repairs) and any decommissioning costs. In some industries, such as the oil industry and civil engineering, sophisticated modelling is used to establish whole-life value, although the approach founders on how value can be defined.
- Job plan and creativity techniques. Using brainstorming approaches, frequently in multi-disciplinary groups, means that many new ideas can be generated quite merely by asking precise questions. Asking 'How can we do this better/faster/cheaper?' or 'How can we apply what we know to a new product or market?' can generate valuable answers in a short time. There is rarely a single, simple, solution to such problems, and these approaches are particularly useful in encouraging creativity in the project team.

LEADING THE ART OF INTERPRETING

Over-optimistic forecasts of likely project performance, based on underestimating aleatoric and epistemic uncertainty in projects, coupled with an over-optimistic assessment of the project team's ability to deal with uncertainty, are significant problems for project decision-making. As we have seen, estimates tend to become commitments that, in turn, become anchors for later decisions. Worse still, people are cognitively hardwired to be optimistic, either for political reasons (getting the project funded or awarded in the first place) or (more often, perhaps) psychologically. We delude ourselves, and we are all complicit with each other in that delusion.

The problem faced by us is that we have to find ways of countering this tendency – of stepping back, looking at the project plan with more realistic, dispassionate eyes and injecting some reality (perhaps even pessimism) into the planning process. We are often unable to be mindful as we are too involved in the 'process' and areas subject to the same cognitive biases as everyone else involved in the work. As a consequence, we must take a leadership role, focusing on people rather than structure and process, taking a longer-term rather than shorter-term view, challenging the status quo and being innovative rather than administrative. Beyond the practical things that can be done to help balance out optimism bias and organisational amnesia, we have a crucial role in shaping the forecasts and avoiding over-simplification of the uncertainty involved in delivering the project.

ASKING INCONVENIENT QUESTIONS

If we can emotionally and structurally detach ourselves from a project (a difficult enough task in itself) we can (as required) slip into the role of devil's advocate that all projects require to combat our tendency to oversimplify. We will be able to challenge the 'inside view' and project an 'outside view' that may be more realistic: prompting our memory, encouraging experts to recall past projects and consider what may go wrong, why it may go wrong and how we could deal with uncertainty. The focus of questioning is to probe limitations in everybody's biased expectations of a future state of a project, and not to question anyone's competence. As inconvenient as these questions may be, they are essential in challenging oversimplification and in encouraging mindful ways of thinking beyond the risk horizon.

OVERCONFIDENCE EFFECT

The overconfidence effect is a cognitive bias observed when people overestimate their ability to do something successfully. Specifically, their subjective confidence in their ability to do something is not borne out by their objective ability (Pallier et al. 2002). There are three distinct ways in which the overconfidence effect can manifest itself. These are:

1. Overestimation of one's actual performance where, for example, someone overestimates their ability to tackle a problem within a specific time limit. Overestimation is a particular problem with complex tasks, although it has also been found that, with simple tasks, people tend to underestimate their abilities. In psychological experiments, this effect was found to form about two-thirds of all manifestations of the overconfidence effect.

2. Overplacement of one's performance relative to others sometimes called the 'better-than-average effect'. A typical example is that when asked about their driving abilities, 90 per cent of people believe themselves to be in the top half. It has been found that this forms a relatively small proportion of instances of the overconfidence effect.

3. Excessive precision in one's beliefs relates typically to people's overconfidence when estimating future uncertainties and usually is found where people are making forecasts about the future in, for example, risk analysis. This particular expression of overconfidence accounts for just under a third of occurrences. (Don Moore and Healy 2008)

Overconfidence in one's ability and knowledge, is a problem that affects people from all walks of life and in all sorts of situations. It has been blamed for everything from the sinking of the Titanic to the Great Recession. In an organisational environment, it is thought that overconfidence is a widespread problem (Healy 2016). It is argued that in complex organisations, people need to stand out to have their ideas considered, and this, in part, leads to overconfident people having undue influence over the direction of organisations. It can be seen in stock market assessments, in estimates of the success of mergers and acquisitions, in the estimates of profit forecasts and in many other aspects of organisational activity.

There are a number of possibilities to explain unwarranted overconfidence. One theory suggests that it is related to the initial best guesses that people then anchor to (Tversky and Kahneman 1974). Other theories suggest that when communicating with others, people prefer being informative to being accurate (Yaniv and Foster 1995), while another theory suggests that overconfidence reflects extremely poor starting point guesses (Moore et al. 2015).

Despite overconfidence being an almost ubiquitous cognitive bias in organisational behaviour, managers can do some things to lessen the effect, as long as they recognise that it is an issue that needs to be considered in decision-making. One strategy is to conduct a 'premortem' (see Chapter 8), where people are asked to list arguments that contradict the reasoning that led to the guess in the first instance. Another approach is to assume the first guess is wrong and then adopt alternative reasoning to derive a second guess. Averaging these two guesses is likely to be more accurate than relying on the first guess alone (Herzog and Hertwig 2009). One more strategy uses the 'wisdom of the crowd'. This approach involves collecting guesses from other stakeholders and using these guesses as the basis of one's own guess (Hogarth 1978).

FOCUSSING ON OPPORTUNITIES

A bias towards the negative side of uncertainty may make us ignore the potential upside in the form of opportunities. We can try and draw attention to how the team could deliver project outputs and outcomes faster, better and cheaper. This is only valid in projects in which deliverables are not set in stone but have incentives for stakeholders to explore and exploit opportunities. It is always valuable to ask the 'Why don't we?' questions, countering loss aversion bias. A positive approach is to establish an entirely separate entity (e.g. a Tiger Team) within the project to break from legacy thinking. Doing this creates different mental and physical spaces to create a balanced view on losses and gains.

DISTINGUISHING BETWEEN NOISE AND 'RELEVANT' UNCERTAINTY

In adopting a dialectic decision-making role, we can encourage a focus on what matters (value); the issue is to distinguish between what matters and what does not. Based on an active reporting culture, we may be bombarded with stakeholders' concerns and flooded with 'what might go wrong' in the project. It is our job to filter out important messages from the abundance of 'noise'. In order not to discourage any report of impending failure, consider all messages as important, though. With the help of the messenger, raise some important questions such as:

- Has this happened before? Is it an indication of aleatoric and epistemic uncertainty?
- Might it influence a part/function of the project that is critical?
- How close have you been to this emerging uncertainty? Do we require more information?
- How quickly could this cascade into a more significant threat?
- What value in a project may it affect?

These kinds of questions can enable effective decisions to be made. We can filter out the less critical uncertainties and concentrate on those that will impact on value. Be sensitive, though, to the idea that the messenger may be conditioned by optimism bias.

MINDFUL PRACTICES

PROJECT MANAGEMENT SOFTWARE

Project Management Software can facilitate the activity of scheduling and estimation. It helps to cope with the abundance of information. Aviva uses commercially available project and portfolio management software as a tool to provide critical information in real-time. This system standardises, manages and captures the execution of project and operational activities and resources. It comprises several modules and components to allow the management of project finances, time recording and resources, including demand, risks and issues.

By using one system to manage multiple functions, the project manager can keep all essential information in a single location that is also available to other team members and is therefore easy to keep up to date:

> *I have found it quite useful – having all the information in one place, and accessible is a real bonus for project managers.*

What is mindful about it? Accessing information is not the only benefit a software tool provides. It should also offer the following:

- Memory: it should be a reminder of the uncertainty and complexity. For example, the system probes the project's commitment to interpreting risk and uncertainty and refreshes participants' ability to do so:

  > *So if you do not review your risks by that date, a report pops up to remind you that you need to review this risk. If you leave it too long, the governance team will pick you up on it and say 'You are not managing your risk, and that will get reported up to your manager.' It's a great incentive to manage risks well and promptly as no-one wants to be seen to be behind.*

- Simplicity: allowing the 'simplification' of data (but be aware of the danger of oversimplification) to aid decision making.
- Nuanced appreciation: it should allow one to distinguish between 'hygiene' factors and novel adversity. Hence, it should help identify patterns across projects and flag up any uncertainty.
- Communication: facilitating instant communication. Timestamps highlight how up-to-date the information is.
- Confidence: providing evidence of the validity of the information. It should help to probe uncertain aspects.
- Challenge: it should not replace the project leader's role in asking inconvenient questions but should help to tackle people's optimism bias.

ADDRESSING THE BIG PICTURE QUESTIONS

Our responsibility as a project leader is not only to challenge people on their perceived degree of certainty, anchored in detailed planning, but also to create a desire in them to be on the lookout for problems, report the possibility of failure and share their perceptions with other members of the project team. In other words, they need to be alert to emerging uncertainty. Alertness, however, requires addressing the 'So What?' question (see Figure 4.2), beyond the boundaries of project tasks.

- **Make choices in the negative.** For everything you decide you want to achieve in a project, articulate what that means you can not do. This forces you to think through the consequences of choosing these options by thinking about what the trade-offs are for each choice you are making.
- **Pretend the project has no money.** When projects are strapped for cash, project decision-makers have to make hard choices about what to spend money on because they do not have enough. It is often during such times that leaders describe themselves as at

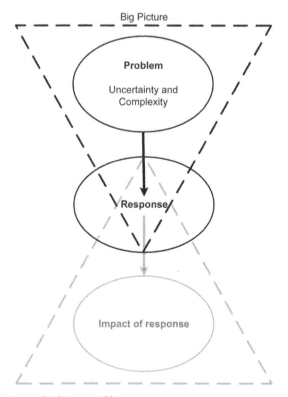

Figure 4.2 *Big picture thinking – problem*

their most strategic. But it is easy to diet if someone's padlocked the fridge – what happens when you get the key back? All too frequently, when the cash starts to flow again, leaders start 'choosing everything' again, and it's this that sows the seeds of the next bout of underperformance. Having too many priorities means you do not really have any, which puts your project's implementation capability under strain. It also compromises your own leadership bandwidth, reducing your ability to macromanage. So pretend you are cash-strapped – it will act as the ultimate constraint on your desire to choose everything.

- **Talk to the unusual suspects.** These could be inside or outside your project, but whoever they are, choose them because they are likely to disagree with you, challenge you, or tell you something you do not know. To ensure you have a ready supply of such

MINDFUL PROJECT MANAGEMENT

people, you may need to look again at your strategic network – it may have gotten too stale to offer you such connections. If that is the case, weed out the deadwood and actively recruit people from different sectors, skill sets, and backgrounds who can help you test the quality of your macro answers. Questions to ask them include: 'Why will this not work?' and 'What do I have to believe for this not to turn out that way?' Being challenged and having new information may well change your answers; even if it does not, it will make your existing answers more robust.

By following these simple mindful steps, we increase the project sensitivity beyond our immediate responsibilities (to be task-focused), enabling and requiring others to see beyond the short-term demands of project delivery and keep in mind what defines value in the project. This is a critical, driving focus that demands a desire to stay alert about uncertainty. It is central to retain the perspective of the Big Picture.

BEING OPTIMISTIC IN THE FACE OF THE ABYSS

It is, of course, vital that we as project leaders stress the potentially imminent nature of uncertainty arising. The project leader must play devil's advocate to inject a dose of the reality of the future unknown to counter over-optimism and curb excessive enthusiasm. Although all this is important if uncertainty is to be meaningfully understood and interpreted within projects, it also poses the danger that the project team may become disheartened and demoralised by a continual preoccupation with adversity. We may feel disempowered in the face of seemingly insurmountable uncertainty where there are no clear resolutions, only half-solutions that satisfy no one. There is a further danger that we may feel nothing we can do will ever allow them to overcome the ever-present uncertainty and that all their effort is pointless. Therefore, another role of us is to guard against a sense of impending fatalism and apathy. The team must be reminded that they are being given capabilities for resilient working in an uncertain and complex environment.

ALLOWING PEOPLE TO APPRECIATE DIFFERENT PERSPECTIVES

Perhaps one of the most prominent early challenges for a project is to find a means of including and capturing the perspectives of multiple stakeholders. This is, of course, entirely dependent on the precise nature of the project being undertaken, but stakeholders rarely speak with one voice, even where they might represent a single organisation. How is the project team to capture and balance the different views of these multiple stakeholders? The project team may well find that these perspectives can be at odds with each other, which risks damaging the project. This is why value-driven project risk management is so important in such a situation. Our role here is to provide the space to make sense of the multiple perspectives at play.

Be careful, though. It is not sufficient to approach these potentially divergent opinions with a view to averaging and normalising them. If we reduce the richness of different perspectives to a single view, a single expectation, a single estimate, we may oversimplify. The abundance of different angles may be captured and used to understand better the nuances of the project so that pragmatic and context-specific solutions can be crafted and shared. Let's appreciate therichness in multiple perspectives without losing sight of the common goal.

Perhaps the most useful starting point is for people to question their own assumptions. This could be done by having a conversation with a cynical colleague or even a person in another organisation – a 'critical friend' who can write down what they think your assumptions are and then confront you with them.

FALSE CONSENSUS EFFECT

The tendency to overestimate the extent to which people agree with us is a cognitive bias known at the false consensus effect, first identified by Ross and sometimes called Ross' False Consensus

Effect (Ross et al. 1977). This agreement could take the form on other peoples' beliefs, values, characteristics, or behaviour. For example, someone with extreme political views might erroneously believe that their views are much more widely held than they are. This might be exacerbated by social media were an algorithm to curate those views with other, similar views giving the person the impression that their opinions and views are widely held. It is thought that the false consensus effect arises because people regard their own views and opinions as normative. Another reason people might be influenced by the false consensus effect is that they tend to generalise from limited case evidence, with their own ideas and views being a data point (Alicke and Largo 1995), known as the availability heuristic.

There are many reasons underpinning the false consensus effect. The first is a self-serving bias – people want to believe their views and opinions are reasonable and prevalent, so they project their opinions on others (Oostrom et al. 2017). Second, our friends, family and colleagues – the people we interact with most often – are likely to be similar to us and share many of our beliefs and opinions, known as selective exposure. Another reason is the result of the egocentric bias – that people see things mostly from their own perspective and so struggle to see things from other peoples' points of view. This can be seen as an anchoring-and-adjustment problem, which leads to the assumed similarity of perspectives. Finally, when context is essential, this exacerbates the false consensus effect. A form of attributional bias, this commonly can be seen where people feel their views are supported by external factors, even where such factors might be aberrant (Gilovich et al. 1983).

Just as people experience the false consensus effect in everyday life, so too do they experience it in organisational life. Typically, the result is prevalent in marketing and promotional contexts. People assume that consumers and other customers will view a product or service in the same way they do. When the product or service is then launched, they are surprised when the market does not respond in the way they expected. The same effect can often be seen in financial analysis and forecasts of future earnings of organisations (Williams 2013).

SEMMELWEIS REFLEX

An interesting cognitive bias is the Semmelweis reflex (sometimes referred to as the Semmelweis effect). It is a propensity of people to reject new ideas or knowledge that contradict prevailing, accepted beliefs and norms. The term refers to the failed efforts of a Hungarian physician, Ignaz Semmelweis, to persuade his colleagues to adopt handwashing as a way of reducing childbed mortality rates. His colleagues experienced a kind of cognitive dissonance and, despite the evidence to the contrary, could not see the benefits of changing their existing practices. While the truth of this story is disputed (or, at least, nuanced) the effect is, nonetheless, a real one.

As with all cognitive biases, the Semmelweis effect can be found in all aspects of daily life, representing inertia to change ingrained habits and behaviours, even when these habits and behaviours are detrimental either to people's own well-being or that of society at large. A good example is people's refusal to accept the evidence of climate change and the need to change their behaviour to combat it.

Within the world of organisations, the Semmelweis reflex can also be found at play. This is often the case where there is an evidenced need for change, but people within the organisation refuse to accept that this is the case. For example, if a once-successful product is failing in the market place and market research suggests there is a problem with the packaging, the Semmelweis reflex might lead managers to reject this evidence out-of-hand and look for an alternative explanation as the packaging was once famous.

EXTENDING THE HALF-LIFE OF UNCERTAINTY

Where project amnesia is present, the experience of uncertainty may quickly fade. This fading can be thought of as the half-life of project learning. We are obligated to extend such memory for as long as possible. In the prolonged absence of failure, and with changes in personnel, this half-life can be remarkably short. Our role in this situation is to employ approaches to prompt memory and retain focus on the possibility of failure, mainly where success has been the norm for a protracted period. Refreshing people's memory of the past while incentivising people to continuously look beyond the risk horizon might seem arduous and detract from the 'actual' work but, without it, patterns of response may be lost over time.

THE IMPACT OF INTERPRETING ON RELATIONSHIPS

A large number of people have only a limited appetite for uncertainty. This is not necessarily good news for our projects. Stakeholders such as funders, sponsors, and end-users all crave for certainty. They want to realise the benefits as soon as possible with a set-out investment of resources. It is incumbent on us not only to demonstrate competence in understanding and being prepared for this but also to disabuse stakeholders of the notion that any project is without such uncertainty, in particular, epistemic uncertainty. It is through this understanding that they will be more able to focus on and draw value from the project. It can be a confusing message to convey, and individuals may not wish to hear it but, if the stakeholders are to avoid delusions of success, it is in their collective interests to engage with this message.

BE RELUCTANT TO COMMIT TO SINGULARITY

Be aware of estimates turning into commitments. If we think about single estimates, we put an 'anchor' in the ground; we expect that estimate to materialise. It is important that uncertainty in estimates is brought to the surface. For example, an estimate can be given with a corresponding confidence level and the use of upper and lower bounds. It is also down to the language that is used to express uncertainty in our predictions. The simple use of 'may' and 'might' provides a necessary – although inconvenient – signpost to stakeholders that project planning is still a look into an unknown future.

Whether the project team is relying on single-point or range-bound estimates, it is essential to note that they are still just estimates. They should not be confused with commitments or constraints, and they should be used with that in mind. Unless this distinction is clear, the results could be painful. This, however, does not mean that estimators can throw caution to the wind and produce completely unreliable numbers. Things to look out for when reporting estimates to a broader stakeholder community are:

- Padded estimates – it is tempting to pad and buffer estimates through building in contingencies and assumptions. Sometimes, this is an appropriate procedure, but in general, it is to be avoided. All it does is create distrust in the overall reliability of the estimates which are, in turn, compromised.
- Failing to revisit estimates – just as the project team should revisit and reassess risk analyses, so too they should continually revisit and reassess estimates. As more information becomes available, so the assumptions and contingencies built into the estimate become more natural to assign.
- Avoid taking estimates at their face value – we tend to be over-optimistic and -confident with our forecasts. It is one of the jobs to find ways of validating and reconciling these estimates before using them as a source for planning or any other decision-making. This is where the role of the devil's advocate or 'critical friend' is important, particularly in tandem with a focus on value.
- Avoid ignoring task dependencies – projects are considered as systems with tasks and activities that have complex interrelationships both within the project and with external systems. These interdependencies introduce uncertainty.

- Communication of estimates – a great deal is at stake in the communication of the estimates. They require the buy-in of influential stakeholders but must also be communicated in such a way that they do not encourage a false certainty.
- Be wary of silos – estimating is not a single person's responsibility, although one individual may be responsible for consolidating and communicating the estimates. Estimating is improved by getting consensus and broader understanding about what we do think we know and what remains unknown, and the more involved the team members are in gathering and discussing the estimates, the richer foresight becomes.

SELLING CAPABILITIES TO DEAL WITH UNCERTAINTY, NOT THE ILLUSION OF CERTAINTY

We are often held up as paragons of planning who can bring control to what might otherwise be chaos. We may come armed with a plethora of techniques and processes, with an idea to instil confidence in stakeholders that we will succeed through careful planning. Perhaps understandably, given the desire for certainty, we may downplay the role of uncertainty in projects. However, it gives a false impression that uncertainty is somehow 'tameable' and can be significantly reduced or even eradicated. Rather than starting on this footing, it might be more useful to form relationships with the stakeholders that acknowledge that uncertainty is ever-present and that the real capability of the project team is to be resilient. In part, this is done through careful planning and control, but it mainly draws on the capabilities of mindful project management. A chief part of this approach is the ability to understand and make sense of uncertainty.

UNDERSTANDING AND APPRECIATING MULTIPLE PERSPECTIVES

Multiple stakeholders bring with them various perspectives of what the project means to them and, moreover, these perspectives are liable to change as the project progresses. Value-driven project management offers

CHAPTER FOUR: THE ART OF INTERPRETING

some techniques that can be used to find and make sense of the value that stakeholders wish to derive from the project. However, this cannot be just a one-off exercise undertaken at the beginning of a project to allow it to proceed. Just as perspectives of value are relational, contextual, and dynamic, so are the attendant uncertainties. If the project team is seeking to understand and meaningfully interpret uncertainty in the project, it needs to be continually attending to the multiple perspectives stakeholders will bring. In this way, it can track and grasp the changing nature of uncertainty as it unfolds through the life of the work.

DEEPWATER HORIZON – A FAILURE OF INTERPRETING

On 20 April 2010, officials of British Petroleum (BP) visited the Deepwater Horizon rig, owned by Transocean and contracted out to BP, and presented the crew with an award for seven years of operating without any personal injuries. On the very same day, at 21:45, high-pressure methane gas expanded up to the wellbore and ignited on the drilling deck, killing 11 workers. The rig sank two days later, resulting in an oil spill and causing the worst environmental disaster in US history.

Deepwater drilling combines a range of challenges such as drilling at depths of up to 3000 m, shut-in pressures of 690 bars, or problematic ground formations. The Deepwater Horizon rig was a 5th generation drilling rig, outfitted with modern drilling technology and control systems. In 2002, it was upgraded with an advanced system of drill monitoring and troubleshooting, including automated shutoff systems.

At the time of the accident, in April 2010, Deepwater Horizon was drilling an exploratory well at the Macondo Prospect. In the wake of the disaster, poorly written emergency procedures and lack of situational awareness were identified as contributing factors. In this respect, a practice called 'inhibiting' was scrutinised.

Inhibit functions are designed to prevent the presentation of warning signals that are deemed inappropriate or unnecessary. In this case, audio or visual warnings could be manually suppressed if an alert was seen as providing unnecessary information or distracting an operator. At Deepwater Horizon, the rig's chief technician, Mike Willaims, observed a culture of inhibiting, whereby control systems are bypassed or, even, shut down. Williams mentioned to investigators:

> When I discovered they [control systems] were inhibited a year ago, I inquired why, and the explanation I got was that from the OIM (the top Transocean official on the rig) on down, they did not want people woken up at 3 a.m. due to false alarms.
>
> (Rong-Gong, Lin 2010)

In the light of cost pressures, the persistence of false alarms combined with the perception of alarms as a nuisance meant that control systems were gradually 'inhibited'; thus, warning signals suppressed and ignored. The rig warning systems tried to alert the operators that a disaster was looming but the alarms went unnoticed.

In project-like work such as deepwater drilling, such technical control systems may well exist, although, in most projects the control system is composed of human beings. If people suffer from optimism bias, effects of normalisation, and reduce the realm of probability to 'It will not happen to me, or will not affect me', then we interpret important warning signals of an impending crisis as just noise that can be easily ignored.

The mindful management of epistemic uncertainty requires scrutiny and scepticism; to take nothing for granted. The focus should be to assume that each signal of failure is an indicator of a more systemic problem that if untreated will cascade into a crisis. A form of discomfort to question, challenge, and scrutinise is of the essence to interpret epistemic uncertainty appropriately.

TOWARDS AN ART OF INTERPRETING

The realistic interpretation of uncertainty is constrained by our longing for simplicity and certainty. We often break down an uncertain environment into its parts and look at them in isolation;

such thinking is amplified by our tendency to underestimate the impact of uncertainty, and to overestimate our capabilities to deal with it. There is help, though. Our desire to make sense of the future through simplification should not be replaced altogether, but it should be challenged. Deploying practices such as a devil's advocate may start us on a journey that challenges our inclination to oversimplify, to interpret a project just within the boundaries of the risk horizon.

Reflection *How well do the following statements characterise your project? For each item, select one box only that best reflects your conclusion.*

	Fully disagree		Neither agree nor disagree		Fully agree
We are reluctant to use single-point estimates.	1	2	3	4	5
We are challenged in our optimism.	1	2	3	4	5
We analyse interdependencies between risks and uncertainties.	1	2	3	4	5

	Fully disagree		Neither agree nor disagree		Fully agree
We appreciate uncertainty beyond the risk horizon.	1	2	3	4	5
We are constantly directed by our value-driven 'big picture'.	1	2	3	4	5
We appreciate that traditional planning tools may amplify oversimplification.	1	2	3	4	5

	Fully disagree		Neither agree nor disagree		Fully agree
We apply practices such as Devil's Advocate.	1	2	3	4	5

	Fully disagree		Neither agree nor disagree		Fully agree
We envisage multiple futures or scenarios.	1	2	3	4	5
We convey to our stakeholders that our project is neither certain nor simple.	1	2	3	4	5

Scoring: Add the numbers. If you score higher than 27, your capability to interpret uncertainty beyond the risk horizon is well developed. If you score 27 or lower, please think about whether you have created an illusion of certainty and control.

REFERENCES

Alicke, M. D., and E. Largo. 1995. "The Role of Self in the False Consensus Effect." *Journal of Experimental Social Psychology* 31(1): 28–47.

Arkes, H. R., and C. Blumer. 1985. "The Psychology of Sunk Cost." *Organizational Behavior and Human Decision Processes* 35(1): 124–40.

Carreyrou, J. 2018. *Bad Blood: Secrets and Lies in a Silicon Valley Startup, by John Carreyrou | Financial Times. Financial Times.* London: Picador.

Flyvjberg, B. 2005. "Design by Deception: The Politics of Megaproject Approval." *Harvard Design Magazine* 22: 50–59.

Gilovich, T., D. L. Jennings, and S. Jennings. 1983. "Causal Focus and Estimates of Consensus: An Examination of the False-Consensus Effect." *Journal of Personality and Social Psychology* 45(3): 550–59.

Healy, P. 2016. "Over-Confidence: How It Affects Your Organization and How to Overcome It." Harvard Business Review Online. 2016. https://online.hbs.edu/blog/post/over-confidence-how-it-affects-your-organization-and-how-to-overcome-it.

Herzog, S., and R. Hertwig. 2009. "The Wisdom of Many in One Mind: Improving Individual Judgments with Dialectical Bootstrapping." *Psychological Science* 20(2): 231–37.

Hogarth, R. M. 1978. "A Note on Aggregating Opinions." *Organizational Behavior and Human Performance* 21(1): 40–46.

Kahneman, D., and D. Lovallo. 2003. "Delusions of Success: How Optimism Undermines Executives' Decisions." *Harvard Business Review* 81(7): 56–63.

Kahneman, D., and A. Tversky. 1991. "Loss Aversion in Riskless Choice: A Reference-Dependent Model." *The Quarterly Journal of Economics* 106(4): 1039–61.

Kutsch, E., H. Maylor, B. Weyer, and J. Lupson. 2011. "Performers, Trackers, Lemmings and the Lost: Sustained False Optimism in Forecasting Project Outcomes – Evidence from a Quasi-Experiment." *International Journal of Project Management* 29(8): 1070–81.

Levine, R. 2006. *The Power of Persuasion: How We're Bought and Sold.* Hoboken, NJ: John Wiley & Sons, Inc.

Moore, D., A. Carter, and H. Yang. 2015. "Wide of the Mark: Evidence on the Underlying Causes of Overprecision in Judgment." *Organizational Behavior and Human Decision Processes* 131: 110–20.

Moore, D., and P. Healy. 2008. "The Trouble with Overconfidence." *Psychological Review* 115(2): 502–17. www.mendeley.com/research/the-trouble-with-overconfidence/.

Oostrom, J. K., N. C. Köbis, R. Ronay, and M. Cremers. 2017. "False Consensus in Situational Judgment Tests: What Would Others Do?" *Journal of Research in Personality* 71: 33–45.

Pallier, G., R. Wilkinson, V. Danthiir, S. Kleitman, G. Knezevic, L. Stankov, and R. D. Roberts. 2002. "The Role of Individual Differences in the Accuracy of Confidence Judgments." *Journal of General Psychology* 129(3): 257–99.

Rick, S. 2011. "Losses, Gains, and Brains: Neuroeconomics Can Help to Answer Open Questions about Loss Aversion." *Journal of Consumer Psychology* 21(4): 453–63.

Rong-Gong, Lin. 2010. "Alarms, Detectors Disabled so Top Rig Officials Could Sleep." Los Angeles Times. 2010. https://www.latimes.com/archives/la-xpm-2010-jul-23-la-oil-spill-disabled-alarms-20100723-story.html.

Ross, L., D. Greene, and P. House. 1977. "The 'False Consensus Effect': An Egocentric Bias in Social Perception and Attribution Processes." *Journal of Experimental Social Psychology* 13(3): 279–301.

Ryan, S. 2016. "How Loss Aversion and Conformity Threaten Organizational Change." *Harvard Business Review Digital Articles* 2–5. 25 November 2016.

Schindler, S., and S. Pfattheicher. 2017. "The Frame of the Game: Loss-Framing Increases Dishonest Behavior." *Journal of Experimental Social Psychology* 69: 172–77.

Shah, P., J. L. Adam, G. B. Harris, C. Catmur, and U. Hahn. 2016. "A Pessimistic View of Optimistic Belief Updating." *Cognitive Psychology* 90: 71–127.

Sharot, T. 2016. *The Optimism Bias: A Tour of the Irrationally Positive Brain.* New York: Pantheon Books.

Sugden, R., J. Zheng, and D. J. Zizzo. 2013. "Not All Anchors Are Created Equal." *Journal of Economic Psychology* 39: 21–31.

Tversky, A., and D. Kahneman. 1974. "Judgment under Uncertainty: Heuristics and Biases." *Science* 185: 1124–31.

Weinstein, N. 1980. "Unrealistic Optimism about Future Life Events." *Journal of Personality and Social Psychology* 39(5): 806–20.

Williams, J. 2013. "Financial Analysts and the False." *Journal of Accounting Research* 51(4): 855–907.

Yaniv, I., and D. P. Foster. 1995. "Graininess of Judgment under Uncertainty: An Accuracy-Informativeness Trade-Off." *Journal of Experimental Psychology: General* 124(4): 424–32.

CHAPTER FIVE

The art of preparing

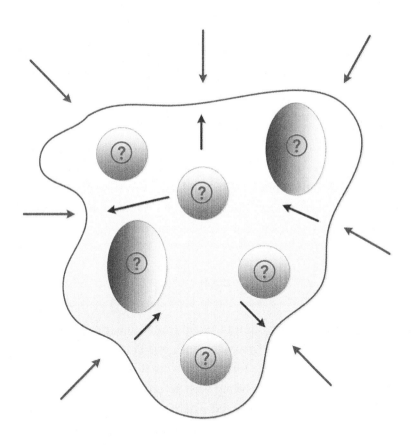

CONTENTS

The mindful organism of a project requires a state of preparedness and readiness to contain adversity. As part of this, project managers need to be innovative in producing novel responses to emerging epistemic uncertainty which, should uncertainty emerge, they can employ to minimise the impacts on the project.

THE LURE OF THE FAIL-SAFE

Planning for adversity often relies on traditional, probabilistic risk management. The risk management process involves identifying aleatoric uncertainty (in the form of risks) that might threaten the delivery of the project and finding ways to reduce or neutralise them. Typically, a process will be enacted whereby risks are identified and strategies put into place to tackle them. These strategies often include finding ways to eliminate the sources of risk, possibly transferring ownership of the problem to someone else (perhaps a supplier) and reducing the possible impact of remaining risks to what might be regarded as acceptable (by putting in place contingency plans). In principle, this is fine; the project can proceed, safe in the knowledge that risk is contained. The key problem with this is that the whole process of preparation and readiness is based on those risks that can be identified. We engage with the project with confidence born of the knowledge that we have conducted a thorough risk management analysis, yet ignorant of the potentially ruinous areas of epistemic uncertainty that we still face – everything beyond the risk horizon. While we have prepared for what we know and understand, we are still vulnerable to the unknown and unexpected.

FIXATION ON PLANNING

Planning provides clear benefits to project management, but planning can also be detrimental if not implemented properly. We may become so fixated on planning for every eventuality in detail that it 'anchors' our expectation to such an extent that it inhibits and stifles creativity and initiative to deviate from a plan and adapt. A detailed plan might be perceived as a 'good' plan, but in essence, turns assumptions and estimates into rigidity in mind and action.

PLANNING FALLACY

Perhaps the most well-known, consistently demonstrated and common cognitive bias found among people, both in everyday life and in organisational life, is the planning fallacy. First identified by Kahneman and Tversky (1979), it has since been the subject of research and investigation (Buehler et al. 1994). The implications, although profound, are still found in all aspects of organisational activity; especially projects (Kutsch et al. 2011).

The planning fallacy mindset refers to the tendency of people to underestimate the time, cost and risk involved in any undertaking, even when they have prior knowledge of exactly what the task will entail (Klayman and Schoemaker 1993). Plans are over-optimistic and often unreasonably mirror the best-case scenario. More specifically, it was found (Kahneman and Tversky 1979) that people predict outcomes of undertakings based only on specific, singular elements of a plan, ignoring distributional data, sometimes called the insider–outsider view. The planning fallacy can be seen in all sorts of everyday experiences such as estimating the time it will take to make a long journey, the time it will take to complete your tax return and so on.

The effects of the planning fallacy tend to be cumulative. The more steps that are involved in planning a task, the more problematic the effect is likely to be. This is because of several reasons. People rarely consider the risk involved in activities or, if they do consider risk, they tend to downplay it (Kutsch et al. 2014). Another reason is that the process of planning involves a future-orientation, which means people are unlikely to consider their past experiences. Even where people do consider the distribution of past experiences, they actively process the information to reduce the pertinence of that information on the planning for the current task (Buehler et al. 1994).

EROSION OF EFFECTIVENESS

Many possible uncertainties will, of course, never materialise. They may never have existed in the first place, or they were mitigated through management. The distinction between 'good' deterministic and probabilistic control and good luck can sometimes be a fine line, though. The preoccupation with control may lead to the temptation to 'cut corners' and reduce the extent of preparations towards the epistemic uncertainty. We dutifully consider the list for a new project, and some risks begin to be relegated. Perhaps these issues have never been experienced in the past, or have not occurred for a long time; maybe we have been involved with a string of successful projects and begin to think that our projects are less uncertain than we first imagined. Clearly, our team is particularly talented – those problems are more likely to affect others, not us. As a result, the nagging doubts fade, confidence grows, in an illusion of certainty. At the same time, pressure on resources encourages us to seek opportunities for greater efficiency. Perhaps one way of freeing up resources, thereby taking the pressure off the budget, is to remove some of the activities directed at protecting the project from these uncertainties that are thought never to have materialised.

OPTIMISM BIAS

Project managers tend to be optimistic. The undertaking of projects demands optimism that difficult and complex objectives can be achieved. Previously we argued that we tend to underestimate the extent of the adversity to which we are exposed. Making matters worse, we may also believe that our preparation covers more possible adversity than it does. As a result, we overestimate our preparatory state. In many respects, adopting a state of optimism is necessary for us. We need to be confident that we can achieve our goals. However, without some reality check, there is a danger that we become overly optimistic about our ability to reach the project's goals, and thus are overconfident in our abilities to address epistemic uncertainty.

BANDWAGON EFFECT

Sometimes called the 'contagion effect', the bandwagon effect is a well-known phenomenon of the general and prevailing opinion impinging upon individuals. What this means is that people tend to take on a view or adopt a behaviour simply because they observe other people doing so. The more people who adopt a behaviour or opinion, the more likely it is that other people will join them (Mutz 1998).

There are many examples of the bandwagon effect that can be observed in everyday life, from fashion trends to musical tastes and from political affiliations to dietary tastes. One more recent example is the take up of different social networking platforms. There are many available, but only a few have risen to prominence.

While the bandwagon effect can be observed, understanding it has been more difficult. Some factors that have been identified are an irrational fear of social isolation and people's desire to be on the winning side. More recently, it has been found that people tend to develop a 'consensus heuristic', taking the majority opinion as the intelligent choice where they lack the expertise to decide for themselves (Mutz 1998). Groupthink is another important factor where there is tremendous pressure to conform to what everyone else is doing. The bandwagon effect also speaks to people's desire to belong to a group, which pressures them to the norms and attitudes of the majority.

There are some severe downsides to the bandwagon effect in society at large and also in organisational life. In society, for example, the growing anti-vaccination phenomenon has, in part, been attributed to this cognitive bias (Hershey et al. 1994). In organisations, the bandwagon effect has been identified as a factor in entry strategies into new markets as well as the adoption of other strategic and operational management 'fads' such as Lean Production techniques and Total Quality management (TQM) (Jung and Lee 2016).

RUNNING ON AUTOPILOT

The 'language' of project management consists to a great extent of written action plans, instructions, and procedures. Articulation is in the form of documents, booklets, and manuals that can sit on a shelf unread and be forgotten about or, increasingly commonly, it resides in databases and on project management information systems. Uncertainty becomes inchoate and opaque. Even if we can be persuaded to engage with the documentation and project management IT systems, they are often perceived as an abstraction from the day-to-day lived reality. Learning, and hence preparation, is arid and lacking in immediacy. There is no sense of getting 'close' to plans. Whereas the execution of plans – the act of containing adversity – stretches our senses and emotions, planning is 'dry' and can be mostly confined to documenting. Planning in all its abstraction does not form an adequate platform for 'really' understanding adversity; of what we know and do not know about the future state of a project.

AUTOMATING A RESPONSE

Project management rigidity is very useful when it comes to imposing stability and discipline. This is often based on an analysis that considers past experiences and documents to be the mandated strategy (usually from recent successes, so this does have some justifiable rationale). The emphasis is on recognised structures, top-down governance and control systems, and prescribed processes and methods. This control is valuable as it ensures that people in the project know what they are doing and do not expose the project to unnecessary adversity through unexpected actions. In this way, the project can indeed be considered as prepared. However, rigidity itself has the potential to become a risk. Backwards-looking procedures and processes stifle the flexibility needed to engage with the novelty and surprise that come with uncertainty. A pragmatic balance is hard to define and articulate within the project.

AUTOMATION BIAS

Automation bias is a cognitive bias that has emerged relatively recently. It is prevalent where automated decision-making tools operate in conjunction with human decision-making. It involves the over-reliance on automated decision support systems that can be found in many different environments (Raja Parasuraman and Manzey 2010). The bias lies in trust in the automated system and the complacency among people that emerges as they rely less on their own or others' inputs.

The kind of highly automated systems that might give rise to automation bias range from complex systems like nuclear control centres and aircraft cockpits to more prosaic examples such as spellcheckers or word processing software. In all cases, people are found to cede some or all their human agency to the automated decision-making tools. Another example is the autopilots for the new breed of electric vehicles (such as Tesla). The autopilot does not truly automate driving but, instead, automates some functions of driving. However, there have been some high profile incidents of people relying on the autopilot functions of these vehicles with, sometimes, catastrophic outcomes.

The problem in organisations is that operatives have been found to be very poor at recognising when the automatic systems they are relying upon have failed and that human intervention is required (Parasuraman et al. 2009). To illustrate this point, there are numerous examples of mistakes and errors being made by, for example, aircraft pilots who rely too heavily on their autopilots.

Technology developers have tried to overcome the problem by giving human operators the final decision in many systems but, even then, it has been found that those operators blithely trust the decision made by the automated system and accept it without checking. In organisations, the effect is to rob people of their critical input into decision-making.

A SILO MENTALITY

To 'defend' a project from adversity, the tendency is often to increase the number of layers within it, both vertically and horizontally. Horizontally, we create silos of specialism and expertise; vertically, we add layers to a hierarchy to have dense, multi-layered defence mechanisms in place. What we tend to forget is that, by doing this, we can add complexity, and hence uncertainty, to the project, and make the project more cumbersome. More silos imply more effort to overcome the inherent barriers, be they defined by specialism, ego, or status. Silos create barriers to communication, in terms of how quickly information gets communicated and in its resultant interpretation by different specialisms. Similarly, specialist groups often form intense, cohesive bonds, which encourage them to protect their own unit from uncertainty, even if this is to the detriment of the overall project. It can create a dangerous 'us and them' attitude.

KEY ENABLERS TO THE ART OF PREPARING

Rigidity and inflexibility, built-in through too detailed planning, are situations we with which we are frequently confronted. This raises some difficult questions. For example, how much planning is actually 'enough'? When does (over)planning become a risk in itself? Although there are no clear answers to these questions, there are some enablers that can be considered in the planning stages to prepare a project for the adversity that comes with, in particular, uncertainty. Preparing for uncertainty is a leap of faith. We must believe that our preparation has some positive effect on containing adversity from destabilising our project. In advance of uncertainty and complexity materialising, there will not be any proof of its effectiveness. Belief and confidence in the effectiveness of your preparation and readiness are therefore paramount.

A WIDE RESPONSE REPOSITORY

One crucial aspect necessary in preparing for epistemic uncertainty is the creation of social redundancy: establishing a wide set of skills and capabilities across the project team that can be focused on any problem that might arise. This involves project staff and workers having to have not only the pertinent skills but also ideally the ability to slot into each other's roles where necessary. This allows the team to develop a comprehensive and active response repository to deploy against any given situation. This is important as, to contain the effects of uncertainty as it emerges, staff need to act quickly and with focus.

Cross-training in a range of skills, beyond individuals' 'core' functions, helps create a built-in redundancy within projects. This excess of skills in the project team may not always be necessary or required (and indeed, it is likely to be a financial expense and possibly a drain on efficiency) until an unanticipated problem arises. It is at this time that the skills become crucial and the value of this investment becomes apparent.

EMPOWERMENT

As shown in Figure 5.1, the more 'traditional' approach to problem-solving is that decision power migrates to different sources of expertise – often defined by hierarchical position or status – until the particular problem is resolved. As a consequence, the nature of the difficulty may need to be conveyed and translated, often resulting in the loss of time and meaning on the way.

An alternative approach is to ensure that the people close to the problem are equipped to deal with it. To do this, they need an extensive response repository to deal with any given problem, be it commercial, legal or technical. Escalations are only necessary when the boundaries of one's skill set are reached. However, in this respect,

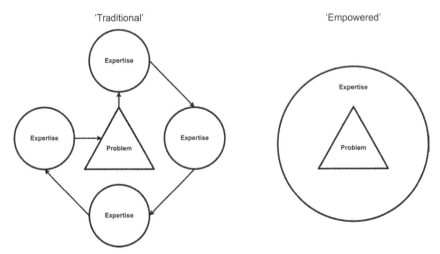

Figure 5.1 *Empowerment beyond specialism*

the number of escalations only shows how restricted one's response repository is. This, in itself, should be seen as a warning signal.

Of course, developing skillsets that span project teams is not easy. It requires the right people with a willingness to be empowered beyond their specialism, expertise and interest. It necessitates investment in training and support and a desire to retain highly skilled individuals. Additionally, simulations, refresher-courses or job-sharing can be crucial in ensuring that skills do not ossify or become obsolete – which in itself leads to additional expenditure.

A by-product of this form of project organising is that project team members with different skills and specialisms can find that they overlap each other. This is the antithesis of the silo mentality – specialisms, status and egos are less likely to get in the way of tackling the problem at hand, and this should benefit the project. This may require us to reconsider the nature of project efficiency. 'Local' efficiency – silos, expertise, tightly controlled work packages – may indeed work well and appear financially prudent, on paper at least. However, 'broader' efficiency in terms of a sufficient response capability may prove superior when difficulties arise and can be resolved more swiftly.

MINDFUL PRACTICES
THE POWER OF EMPOWERMENT

You are given a lot of responsibility, but you are also given a lot of freedom ... you don't have managers telling you on a daily basis what to do; each person decides themselves what needs to be done.

Project managers at TTP are empowered to make decisions regarding product development and customer service. The extent of responsibility and authority are given to them can be breath-taking. From the 'cradle to the grave' of a project, managers are not simple executors of project management activities but take on a whole variety of roles, such as commercial, legal, and project 'ownership', regardless of their original specialism. Such empowerment is by no means a comfortable proposition:

Oh, it is very scary, even now, even today.

The benefits of empowerment are manifold, though. Project managers have a greater sense of purpose due to their extensive responsibility to look at a project from new and unfamiliar perspectives. This unfamiliarity, despite being uncomfortable, has the benefit of increasing their alertness and attention to problems that otherwise might remain hidden. Managers who extend their repertoire instead of delegating it to 'experts' see a situation with fresh eyes. They perceive more and are thus better positioned to notice and contain issues before they cascade into a crisis.

Seeing more and being able to put it together as a big-picture helps to maintain oversight of project performance. It helps to address the issue of risk blindness that is so often a problem of centralised and 'specialist' project organisations. Going hand-in-hand with greater alertness and vigilance concerning the unexpected, project managers at TTP feel firmly attached to their projects and their organisation. Not only is their expertise valued but so are their skills in going beyond their expertise and initiative to push the envelope beyond what they are comfortable with.

It is acknowledged at TTP that there needs to be a balance between empowerment and traditional management. Empowerment, as valuable as it might be, comes with potential challenges. A few find the responsibility overwhelming (and may leave). Senior management at TTP has to be sensitive to the needs of project managers as well as to the needs of the company and to know how to use a management style that will work best to achieve the desired outcomes. The principle of 'letting go' does not occur in a vacuum. A supportive culture (not to be confused with the traditional 'command and control' style) at TTP provides a 'safe' environment in which the responsibility of empowerment resting on a project manager's shoulders should not become a burden and a constraint.

What is mindful about it? The benefits of empowering are manifold: higher job satisfaction, a greater sense of purpose and a greater incentive to engage with uncertainty beyond the risk horizon. A fundamental benefit of empowerment is the process by which we access knowledge, capabilities, skills, and resources to enable us to gain control over uncertainty. In other words, as empowered project members, we are more inclined to see a project through 'fresh eyes': raising questions otherwise not asked, challenging ourselves and others, or acting upon uncertainty instead of 'escalating' it away from us.

SIMULATIONS, GAMES, REHEARSALS

Just as airline pilots simulate many possibilities before getting into a real cockpit for the first time, so too should we rehearse how to manage a project before we engage with it. The underlying purpose of a simulation is to shed light on the mechanisms that control the behaviour of a project. More practically, simulations can be used to predict (forecast) the future behaviour of a project and determine what might be done to influence that future behaviour. This is not to be mistaken with predicting or forecasting the future. It is about 'testing' how the project team operate under conditions that might be expected in the 'reality' of project delivery. Naturally, a simulation will vary from context to context and project to project, but simulations focused on the unexpected and hitherto unexperienced possibilities, are entirely feasible in almost all project settings.

Understanding our capabilities as a project team to engage with uncertainty, in a safe environment, can be achieved through various means, such as project management simulations, but also role-plays or exercises which stretch our senses about our way of working. In this respect, most project teams, unfortunately, prepare and ready themselves through overly abstract, detailed planning that fosters rigidity and inflexibility.

ROUTINE-FLEXIBILITY

Routines, the possible outcome of too detailed planning and the temptation to run a plan on autopilot, are valuable in stable, secure and repeatable environments in that they ensure consistency in managing uncertainty. However, many projects are often anything but stable. The idea of imposing rules and procedures on an environment in flux may be counterproductive. A way of limiting flux and creating the conditions for stability is to try to close the project off from outside influences. However, protecting it from changes by stakeholders and keeping uncertainty out may also mean inhibiting the possibility of enhancing value. For example, 'protecting' the project might mean preventing stakeholders, such as end-users, from getting involved in explaining what they want, especially when the project is underway. So, although boundaries (see Figure 5.2) around the project might protect the key deliverables by limiting opportunities for change, they also mean that the project is less likely to deliver precisely what the end-users actually need. If sponsors and funders are to draw maximum value from the project, then they will have to require project teams to allow them to get involved. This, in turn, exposes the project to the possibility of ongoing change and with that comes additional uncertainty. Rigid routines may collapse in this kind of environment, so what is required in projects is a degree of flexibility to adjust to the possibility of an ever-changing environment.

Flexibility, though, can be detrimental to project performance. Too much can become counterproductive, so project teams require latitude to be flexible yet must not lose sight of the rules and procedures that allow the project to keep on track. This concept was articulated at Harley Davidson and is sometimes known as 'freedom with fences'

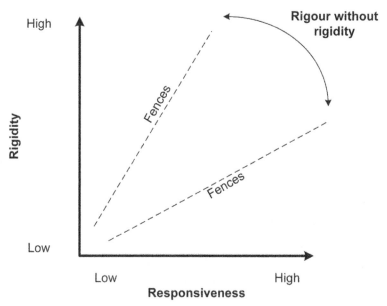

Figure 5.2 *Freedom with fences*

(Stenzel 2010). By adopting this approach, project members not only have the freedom to 'push back' where this might be required, but this very flexibility itself should become a routine, a kind of (dynamic) capability. Flexibility itself becomes the routine mindset. This approach needs to be understood and embedded in the mindset of the project team from the start, meaning that whenever uncertainty emerges, we are immediately able to loosen our 'normal' operating practices and respond with innovative and imaginative solutions and ways of working.

In this way, routine-flexibility is not the contradiction in terms that it may at first seem to be. Routines are produced by many people with different preferences, amounts of information and interpretations. This situation provides scope not only for stability but also for flexibility and change within organisations. Routines are the default position and provide boundaries within which flexibility can be exercised. Essentially, it is a matter of releasing the flexibility aspect and allowing it free rein, but within defined constraints: 'fences'. Patrolling the fences (the limits of freedom) is the job of the project leader, who takes a strategic perspective on the project goals and ensures that changes enacted within the project in the face of uncertainty do not unduly threaten the project outcomes.

A SENSIBLE PLANNING HORIZON

Given that a planning process will be undertaken in almost all projects, a vital issue will be how far we venture beyond the risk horizon. The risk horizon is defined by detailed, articulated, and actionable plans. The problem with thinking and acting too far out the risk horizon is one of fantasising: imagining a remote future that we hope, expect, or fear to happen, or preparing and readying us for a future that is so lofty that it provides no reference of a future at all.

Preparing and readying ourselves for thinking and acting beyond the risk horizon involves a discussion of how much we want to embrace the unknown. The question of how much stakeholders are willing to sensibly embrace the unknown beyond the risk horizon is only a starting point.

GOAL FLEXIBILITY

One aspect of uncertainty that sometimes gets forgotten is the alternative view of uncertainty as opportunities. Instead of just considering the negative implications, it can make sense to seek flexibility in the project goals and try to turn threats into opportunities. For example, regular planning iterations allow goals to be reassessed repeatedly, expectations to be managed, and learning from previous iterations to be incorporated. Each iteration is allowed to influence the next, and this process is quite transparent. This ability to be flexible with targets allows both for risks to be addressed and for opportunities to be incorporated. This is not suitable for every project, but even where stakeholders are quite clear on the outcomes and benefits they want from the work, a door remains open to adjusting those goals in light of uncertainty.

LEADING THE ART OF PREPARING

We need to be prepared and ready to deal with whatever might happen. We need to be vigilant in looking for uncertainties as they begin to emerge, alert to threats, and alive to opportunities. It is both confusing and counterproductive to seal the project off from its environment in the hope of 'keeping uncertainty out', and equally problematic (and more than likely, ineffective) to tighten rules and procedures in the hope of eliminating project failure.

Preparation commonly begins with standard risk procedures (routines) being put in place, but it is dangerous to leave things there in the hope that this covers all eventualities. The risk register should be just a starting point. It is incumbent on us to create a sense of preparedness and readiness among the project team so that they are not just ready for the expected but appreciate the threat of the unexpected, the unknown. This means empowering the project team, providing the freedom and latitude to act, and creating a culture of communication by removing the barriers that might prevent this, thereby enhancing flexibility. It also means, incentivising and rewarding project members to be constantly on the lookout for emerging uncertainty and committed to act upon it.

MINDFUL PRACTICES
TRAINING

Project management training is often related purely to conveying hard skills, such as how to apply processes and procedures. Although such training is beneficial and provides a project leader at TTP with a set of tools, TTP's 'Project Leadership Programme' also emphasises the soft side of leading a project:

The project leadership course is opening people's eyes to the tools that are available to them to deal with things and actually also their freedom to use them, not to assume constraints but actually they can make a difference ...

The 'hard' focus of training involves familiarisation with traditional 'waterfall' planning approaches such as Gantt charts and risk management. However, most of the time is spent on contextualising:

- leadership;
- conflict management;
- stakeholder/relationship management;
- time management;
- motivation.

Of great importance in this leadership programme is how it is conveyed, and a variety of methods are used to present learning material. These include TTP-specific case studies, role-playing, exercises and in-class simulations. This maintains the attention of training participants. Feedback is provided regularly, and participants engage in the exchange of ideas with each other and the facilitators. The training programme is divided into small 'doses', so delegates do not become overwhelmed. Acquired knowledge is then immediately applied in the form of interactive training sessions. Finally, a key factor is that the training programmes are designed to be exciting and entertaining.

What is mindful about it? The project management profession is often characterised as being trained in deterministic and probabilist planning techniques, enabling project managers to apply a project management framework (or body of knowledge) consistently. However, this training is unlikely to lead to a mindset of mindfulness and, thus, project managers are unlikely to be alert to epistemic uncertainty. In fact, the opposite is likely to be the case; an overreliance on consistency in action, informed by tools designed to predominantly address aleatoric uncertainty can reinforce mindless behaviour, however efficient it may be.

Training in the management of epistemic uncertainty can lead to greater awareness, inquisitiveness and more creativity and mental

engagement with epistemic uncertainty. As a consequence,
soft-skills training, focusing on adaptive leadership, team
improvisation and constructive conflict management may be
a good start of training to project managers.

MAINTAINING GOAL FLEXIBILITY

If project iterations are implemented, a key aspect is not merely to
progress to the next iteration but to ensure that a short phase of
reflection occurs. Seeking to learn from the previous output and
considering how this may influence the overall goal is valuable. These
short but intense reflection periods may include questioning how
the experience of the completed iteration affects the project delivery
process and what that means for the overarching project goal. It is a
reflection of how the creation of value (see Chapter 4) evolves. As a
result, it is essential to communicate and sensitise people to the idea
that nothing is set in stone and that the learning from an iteration
informs subsequent iterations.

EMPOWERING PROJECT MEMBERS

Exhorting us to empower workers and staff to act on their own
initiative can be difficult. There are two general problems: that we
are reluctant to lose what we perceive as control; and that project
members are unwilling to take responsibility. From the leader's point
of view, a transformational model can be far more effective than a
transactional model. Transactional leaders focus primarily on role
supervision, organisation and compliance, paying attention to work
performed to spot faults and deviations. Transformational leaders focus
more on being a role model, inspiring and keeping workers interested,
challenging others to take greater ownership for their work, and
understanding their strengths and weaknesses.

For transformational project leaders, empowerment can be promoted in several ways:

- To encourage on-the-spot feedback so that issues are communicated quickly and action can be taken immediately. The ground rules for such feedback need to be clearly set – it must be both constructive and respectful. Fundamentally, the project team must trust its leader and each other to deliver honest and helpful praise and criticism.
- To provide the empowered project actor with an abundance of expertise to allow the most informed decision making. In this respect, expertise is not supposed to 'take over' decision making but to support, guide, question and challenge.
- Project leaders can adopt an 'executive mentality' and approach. Hosting regular meetings with their teams and sharing with them the happenings within the organisation help the teams understand the main goals they are driving towards. Giving them a rundown on how other projects or parts of the organisation are performing makes it easier for them to adopt this mindset.
- It is crucial to present project workers with new challenges and stretch-assignments so they can demonstrate and achieve their full potential.
- Although project members should be encouraged to embrace new experiences, they cannot be pushed too far out of their comfort zones or the experience will become a negative one. Their boundaries must be respected. It is the job of the project leader to recognise and understand this.
- Empowered project members need to have some control over how they direct their work. This means having the freedom to express flexibility and creativity. It also means that project workers will act on their own initiative, but this flexibility needs to be within limits (freedom with fences), which must be explained to project staff.
- Giving up control and empowering a project team might feel like a very uncomfortable experience for many project leaders who are used to a more transactional model of control and compliance. The temptation is to watch the workers' every move but, in

monitoring someone closely, their ability to grow, learn, and build confidence to take action is impeded. The project workers need to be given space and need to be trusted.

REACTANCE

Psychological reactance is the deep-seated and instantaneous reaction all people feel to being told they have to do something. This manifests itself as an unpleasant feeling people experience when they think they will lose their freedom to act (Brehm and Brehm 1981).

Examples of threats to the freedom to act can be found in all walks of life. For example, being persuaded to buy a specific product, being instructed to visit the doctor, being prohibited from using a mobile phone or being instructed to perform some task for someone in authority can all lead to psychological reactance. This can take the form of resistance (simply refusing to perform the task) all the way to purposely doing the opposite of what was ordered, seemingly to spite the one in authority giving the instruction. The extent of the reactance has been found to depend on the perceived importance of freedom under threat and the magnitude of the threat.

Reactance is very commonly observed in organisations, principally as a resistance to change being imposed on people. This has been found to manifest itself in numerous ways and acts at the level of the individual as well as the group (Nesterkin 2013).

BREAKING DOWN BARRIERS

The way to break down barriers between silos is twofold. First, we should try and reduce the number of hierarchical levels, so that communication can flow more rapidly. Think of the flattest hierarchy possible. Second, empowerment in itself reduces the need for in-depth silos of expertise. Instead, 'wider' silos with extended insight and responsibility can be created. 'Generalists' can work as effective conduits of expertise between specialists, since they have broader (but shallower) domain knowledge and can be useful 'boundary-spanners'.

This, though, is a rather structural option to breaking down barriers, which may take more subtle, behavioural forms. Culturally, egos and status may prevent the rapid flow of information. One way to overcome this is to work so that decision-making is driven by those who are the closest to the problem and have the most considerable expertise to deal with it.

In terms of geographically distributed (or virtual) teams, it is essential to promote some social interaction. Encourage people to meet or, if that is not possible, at least try to make sure they can see each other. Personal, real-time communication helps build trust and effective working relationships between non-co-located staff.

HELPING PEOPLE TO GET 'CLOSE' TO UNCERTAINTY

We tend to be comfortable investing significant resources in ensuring that computer simulations are carried out on the technical aspects of engineering projects, especially where there is a risk of catastrophic failure that could lead to loss of life or high cost. As a result, engineering elements are carefully designed and rarely fail. However, the kind of simulations, role-playing and games that would be useful to prepare project members for the 'soft' risks of stakeholder interaction and behaviour are rarely undertaken outside a business school environment. Even where training like this does occur, it usually is in a sterile classroom setting.

We are responsible for ensuring that the project team is prepared and ready to tackle uncertainty and one way of preparing them is to undertake simulations, role-plays and games that allow you to experience and 'feel' the management of uncertainty. Although it is often tricky, we should try to find the time and resources to ensure that the project team has the opportunity to participate in these kinds of simulations and, in so doing, gets 'close' to how we work with each other in a tangible and memorable way, before we plan the project.

Role-plays, in particular, can fill participants with dread but some simple procedures can help ensure that the whole process goes smoothly and that the participants feel they are learning and getting close to risk and uncertainty. These are:

- *Objectives*. It needs to be clear about why the role-play is being undertaken, whether it is being assessed in some way and whether the activity is being tailored for different skills and experience.
- *Timing*. Is the role-play to be a one-off experience or is it part of a broader risk analysis/management activity? Frequently, it is held at the end of a training session or management activity with the idea that participants are then able to apply lessons learnt.
- *Briefing*. We need to be clear about what they are supposed to do. This should be supported by sufficient time to prepare, rather than just being rushed into a scenario.
- *Observation and feedback*. Observers can be hugely beneficial to participants' learning and observation should be encouraged.

In summary, role-play events should be focused and clear. The participants should be able to see the relevance to their project and take their learning back to the workplace.

INCENTIVISING BEYOND COMPLIANCE

The reward and incentive scheme has to reinforce the open flow of communication required of the project team as well as support an open and ongoing discussion of project purpose. There are some techniques we can utilise to encourage the kind of focus required (Roberts et al. 2001):

- Use interviews and focus groups to ensure the real goals of the project are understood and shared.

- Review the reward and incentive procedures from the standpoint of balancing compliance to a framework with the adaptive capacity to deviate from a rule-based approach to project management.
- Develop and reward uncertainty identification activities and include these in staff evaluation.

The reward and incentive process needs to focus on both the intrinsic and extrinsic motivation of a project team to engage with epistemic uncertainty in a mindful manner. Providing project members with greater autonomy and latitude to act, with fewer process and procedural constraints are in itself a powerful intrinsic motivator. Extrinsic rewards are in terms of financial and status outcomes. This reward system should be focused on communication and vigilance – supporting resilience – rather than just on speedy, efficient activity which may be too focused on the smaller, short-term picture.

SELF-SERVING BIAS

A widespread cognitive bias, the self-serving bias involves taking the credit when things go well and blaming external factors when things go badly. It is so commonplace because it speaks to our own self-esteem. People can increase their confidence and self-esteem by attributing positive events to personal characteristics, while at the same time they can both protect their self-esteem and avoid taking personal responsibility if they blame outside forces for their failures (Larwood and Whittaker 1977).

There are many examples that can be found in everyday life. For instance, in a car accident the drivers might blame each other. Similarly, if a student does well in an exam, they may attribute this to hard work and dedication, whereas if they do poorly, they may blame poor teaching or distractions during the exam.

In organisations, self-serving bias can create a host of problems. For example, where people are looking to understand the results of actions, this can be undermined if they blame other factors for things going wrong. The result is that capability failings may not be addressed. Where organisations are developing risk plans, they are more likely to acknowledge external risks than to consider risks that might be generated from within the organisation. The same goes for security systems, where organisations are more likely to guard against external threats and downplay threats from within. Another example involves control mechanisms within organisations. As controls are developed by managers, these are more likely to focus on controlling the employees being managed than the behaviours and actions of the managers themselves.

THE IMPACT OF PREPARING ON RELATIONSHIPS

The preparations for delivering a resilient project are not necessarily confined to the immediate project team. Any suppliers or contractors also need to be brought into the preparation processes. One aspect of preparation is dealing with the issues of power and politics. For this, attention also needs to be turned to other stakeholders: funders; sponsors; possibly end-users – in short, those stakeholders who could be particularly influential. As much as we need to be prepared for uncertainty that may arise as the project progresses, so too other stakeholders must be made aware that they themselves are a source of that uncertainty. They should be encouraged to focus on the 'big picture' as much as the little details, and also be alert to the weak, early signs of materialising uncertainty.

ENGAGING STAKEHOLDERS IN PREPARATIONS

Just as the project team should be involved in preparations for resilience, so too should key stakeholders. In many ways, the same issues apply – they need to guard against complacency, be ready to be flexible and to let go of constraining procedures when uncertainty emerges. They might legitimately ask why they need to worry about all these issues of preparation towards uncertainty. The principal way of encouraging involvement in the process of addressing uncertainty is through appropriate incentives, which again should not focus on only simple task completion but more so on the mindful ability to adapt to materialising uncertainty.

MINDFUL PRACTICES
ESTABLISHING LONG-TERM COMMITMENT

Projects are temporary endeavours and so too is the commitment to them. Engagement and dedication often do not extend beyond the duration of the work as people move on. Frequently, short-term and, in particular, long-term outcomes of a project become forgotten or are scrutinised by outsiders such as external assessors (whose expertise the project participants may question) who were not involved in the delivery of the project.

Aviva has sought to overcome this. The typical detachment and lack of long-term commitment to a project are countered by committing critical decision-makers to the long-term benefits beyond the duration of their project implementation. It all starts with the sponsor. A sponsor at Aviva is a functional manager – usually a director – for whom the project is expected to have a positive effect. The sponsor will bid for a project by developing a business case, to be scrutinised by an independent panel:

> *The idea of the bank manager model is that if someone wants a project to happen, they need to be prepared to sponsor it but not just for the short term of getting that project up and running and implemented but also for at least two years after implementation so that the benefits are realised.*

Such a business case outlines the traditional short-term outputs of a project (i.e. time, budget, specification) but also asks the sponsor to define outcomes that should apply two years after the end of the project. Some examples of these outcomes might include:

- increased efficiency in operations;

- reduction of legal vulnerability;

- improved public image.

The sponsor and the project manager share a collective responsibility to deliver both project outputs and outcomes, as they are intrinsically built on each other. Challenges are jointly addressed by the project manager and sponsor:

> *So, for example, if I [as the project manager] suddenly hit a brick wall on my project, and I need extra resources, and all the IT teams are saying to me we don't have any additional resources, then I'll go to my sponsor and explain that if the delivery is to continue, they will need to intervene to sort the issue out.*

They tend to be measured subjectively by approximation. To address uncertainty in estimating these outcomes, some are defined with the help of approximations such as ranges (from-to).

At Aviva, the sponsor is committed to the longer-term, often difficult to measure, outcomes while the project manager concentrates on delivering the more specific short-term outputs. In particular, this arrangement drives the engagement of the sponsor in the project as well as in transferring short-term outputs into long-term outcomes. This form of engagement is further underlined by the impact of not achieving (or exceeding) initially defined outputs and outcomes. Both the sponsor's and the project manager's future prospects, including the type of projects they can sponsor or manage, are in play and there is an emphasis on incentivising the exploitation of opportunities to deliver something better, faster and at less cost next time:

There will be an impact on what sorts of things they're allowed to sponsor or manage in the future ...

What is mindful about it? Due to uncertainty, inherent in any project, those unmet short-term objectives may drive a wedge between stakeholders and the project delivery team, unless goal flexibility allows a project to change the goalposts in line with what is defined as value by stakeholders. Mindful project management involves a long-term commitment, beyond the risk horizon, towards attainable long-term goals. Mindful foresight beyond the risk horizon focuses one's attention beyond the iron-triangle, beyond short-term goals cost, budget and meeting specifications. This attention drives a commitment to longer-term achievements and puts unmet short-term goals into a perspective of long-term benefits.

To drive long-term commitment, the project sponsor is primarily concerned with ensuring that the project delivers the agreed upon business benefits and acts as the representative of the organisation, playing a vital leadership role through a series of areas:

- Provides business context, expertise, and guidance to the project manager and the team.
- Champions the project, including 'selling' and marketing it throughout the organization to ensure capacity, funding, and priority for the project.
- Acts as an escalation point for decisions and issues that are beyond the authority of the project manage.
- Acts as an additional line of communication and observation with team members, customers, and other stakeholders.
- Acts as the link between the project, the business community, and strategic level decision-making groups.

ADDRESSING DISCOMFORT

Goal flexibility and the commensurate implications of epistemic uncertainty for the planning process may well be uncomfortable for stakeholders. The idea of ever-shifting goalposts and using diverse ways to accomplish the project is difficult to justify. If not addressed, there is a possibility that the project manager will be labelled a 'bad' planner. Stakeholders need to understand why the planning horizon is shortened and need to be guided through the logic. We should offer advice, transparency and clarity about the planned state of a project, as well as about what we are not clear about.

MINDFUL PRACTICES
WINNING HEARTS AND MINDS

The commitment of stakeholders to buy into a project and, importantly, into the uncertainty attached to it, is not solely driven by the project brief or by a contract that has been signed off. Central to committing people to a project is trust and respect:

> *Usually [we listen to] their questions, their concerns, their objections and often it boils down to the fact that they didn't really understand why they were being asked to do it and they didn't have time. So you find them some resource, you help them have the time, you talk to the manager if necessary and get them the time but more importantly you make sure they understand why they're doing this because if they understand it, even if they do not totally agree with it, they're more likely to do it.*

Listening to, and understanding, stakeholders' objectives and concerns and managing their need to have a greater understanding of what the project is, is all about helping to ensure that everyone is on the same page. The project leader delivering that message must:

- allow time to listen to stakeholders, being careful not to cut off a discussion because of other obligations;
- allow face-to-face conversation and personal interaction to allow social bonding;
- minimise external distractions by focusing attention on what is being said;
- keep an open mind;
- ask questions to clarify and to show enthusiasm about the message and the messenger.

Listening, *per se*, makes Aviva stakeholders 'worthy' – appreciated, of interest and valued. This is paid back as openness towards what the project stands for and how it affects them. However, listening needs to be followed by converting this openness into trust, a belief that the message – the project – is for the good of oneself *and* other beneficiaries. This depends upon credibility being established by providing honest feedback on the discussions. 'How are concerns addressed?', 'How can objectives be aligned?', 'What questions help build up credibility?' At Aviva, the action of establishing credibility is supported by 'evidence', be it benchmarks, case studies, or comparable projects where something similar has worked. Working together and finding compromises helps build credibility and allows trust to blossom.

What is mindful about it? A project is ultimately a social undertaking. Any project success, in the short- or long-term is down to the extent of social cohesion between stakeholders. Social cohesion works toward the well-being of project members; it fights exclusion and marginalisation, creates a sense of belonging, and most importantly builds trust within the project team in an environment that is inherently uncertain. Previously mentioned suggestions about role plays, simulations, and the use of devil's advocates might all contribute to social cohesion, and thus contribute to task cohesion. This influences the degree to which stakeholders of a project might work together to achieve common goals. Social cohesion as the extent to which people in society are bound together and integrated and share common values is the bedrock of mindful project management!

SPACE SHUTTLE COLUMBIA – A FAILURE OF PREPARING

The Space Shuttle programme was the fourth programme of human spaceflight at the National Aeronautics and Space Administration (NASA), relying on a reusable spacecraft and solid rocket boosters as well as a disposable external fuel tank. The Space Shuttle could carry up to eight astronauts and a payload of up to 23 t to a low Earth Orbit. The fatal mission of the Columbia was designated STS-107, and was the 113th Space Shuttle launch since the inaugural flight on 12 April 1981 (STS-2).

On 1 February 2003, the Space Shuttle Columbia disintegrated, with the loss of the entire crew. After the 1986 Challenger disaster, it was the second fatal accident in the Space Shuttle programme that considerably tarnished the reputation of NASA.

During the launch of the Space Shuttle Columbia on 16 January, a piece of thermal foam insulation broke off from the external tank and struck the reinforced carbon panels of Columbia's left wing. The resulting hole allowed hot gases to enter the wing upon re-entrance to Earth's atmosphere.

The Columbia Accident Investigation Board delved into NASA's organisational and cultural shortcomings that led to the accident. A key issue was excessive pride or self-confidence of NASA in their readiness and preparedness to manage uncertainty:

*The Von Braunean dedication to flawless performance was replaced
by an emphasis on efficiency during President Nixon's term in office.
At about the same time, NASA also implemented a hierarchical
decision structure that separated decision making into levels and
accorded substantial power to decision-makers at the top level. Many
managers operating in this new arrangement lulled themselves into
believing that NASA's early successes were due to the agency's – and
perhaps their – invulnerability.*

(Mason 2004, 134)

In projects, repeated successes breed complacency in ones
'invulnerability', underlined by the lure of the fail-safe. To address
such hubris, we need to remind ourselves that epistemic uncertainty
remains prevalent and that we may be mindless in our appreciation
of uncertainty. Also, the discomfort of not knowing what the future
holds goes hand in hand with an incentive to establish mindful
capabilities that allow a project to adapt to a changing situation
by empowering front-line employees and providing tools and
techniques to look beyond the risk horizon, but more so to act
beyond it.

TOWARDS AN ART OF PREPARING

This chapter has been about resisting the temptation to prepare a
project for a single, most likely future. Uncertainty means that
this is unwise. Instead, a project needs to be ready for multiple futures,
accepting the uncertainty that lies beyond the risk horizon. Providing
an extensive repository of options, empowering people beyond their
specialisms, breaking down barriers and silos between people, and
the integrative role of stakeholders in exploiting this flexibility is
paramount. Hence, resilience is not just an outcome of accurate and
precise planning for the expected; it is an outcome of preparing a
project for epistemic uncertainty.

Reflection *How well do the following statements characterise your project? For each item, select one box only that best reflects your conclusion.*

	Fully disagree		Neither agree nor disagree		Fully agree
We believe in the effectiveness of our management of uncertainty, although we have no proof about what we do not know with confidence.	1	2	3	4	5
The goal of the project is not set in stone but can be influenced by what we learn throughout the project.	1	2	3	4	5
We experience uncertainty before it happens, and do not just plan for it.	1	2	3	4	5

	Fully disagree		Neither agree nor disagree		Fully agree
Project members have an extensive skill set that enables them to act on uncertainty.	1	2	3	4	5
We are equipped with wide-ranging freedom to act, beyond process.	1	2	3	4	5
We are trained beyond our specialism.	1	2	3	4	5

	Fully disagree		Neither agree nor disagree		Fully agree
People can rely on each other without any barriers to overcome.	1	2	3	4	5

	Fully disagree		Neither agree nor disagree		Fully agree
We share the discomfort of uncertainty with our stakeholders.	1	2	3	4	5
Our stakeholders are part of the preparation.	1	2	3	4	5

Scoring: Add the numbers. If you score higher than 27, your preparedness beyond the risk horizon is good. If you score 27 or lower, please think of how you can enhance your state of preparedness in regards to epistemic uncertainty.

REFERENCES

Brehm, S. S., and J. W. Brehm. 1981. *Psychological Reactance: A Theory of Freedom and Control*. New York: Academic Press.

Buehler, R., D. Griffin, and M. Ross. 1994. "Exploring the 'Planning Fallacy': Why People Underestimate Their Task Completion Times." *Journal of Personality and Social Psychology* 67(3): 366–81.

Hershey, J. C., D. A. Asch, T. Thumasathit, J. Meszaros, and V. V. Waters. 1994. "The Roles of Altruism, Free Riding, and Bandwagoning in Vaccination Decisions." *Organizational Behavior and Human Decision Processes* 59(2): 177–87.

Jung, D. I., and W. H. Lee. 2016. "Crossing the Management Fashion Border: The Adoption of Business Process Reengineering Services by Management Consultants Offering Total Quality Management Services in the United States, 1992–2004." *Journal of Management and Organization* 22(5): 702–19.

Kahneman, D., and A. Tversky. 1979. "Intuitive Prediction: Biases and Corrective Procedures." *TIMS Studies in Management Science* 12: 313–27.

Klayman, J., and P. J. H. Schoemaker. 1993. "Thinking about the Future: A Cognitive Perspective." *Journal of Forecasting* 12(2): 161–86.

Kutsch, E., H. Maylor, B. Weyer, and J. Lupson. 2011. "Performers, Trackers, Lemmings and the Lost: Sustained False Optimism in Forecasting Project Outcomes – Evidence from a Quasi-Experiment." *International Journal of Project Management* 29(8): 1070–1081.

Kutsch, E., T. R. Browning, and M. Hall. 2014. "Bridging the Risk Gap: The Failure of Risk Management in Information Systems Projects." *Research Technology Management* 57(2): 26–32.

Larwood, L., and W. Whittaker. 1977. "Managerial Myopia: Self-Serving Biases in Organizational Planning." *Journal of Applied Psychology* 62(2): 194–98.

Mason, R. O. 2004. "Lessons in Organizational Ethics from the Columbia Disaster: Can a Culture Be Lethal?" *Organizational Dynamics* 33(2): 128–42.

Mutz, D. C. 1998. *Impersonal Influence: How Perceptions of Mass Collectives Affect Political Attitudes*. Cambridge, UK: Cambridge University Press.

Nesterkin, D. A. 2013. "Organizational Change and Psychological Reactance." *Journal of Organizational Change Management* 26(3): 573–94.

Parasuraman, R., and D. H. Manzey. 2010. "Complacency and Bias in Human Use of Automation: An Attentional Integration." *Human Factors* 52(3): 381–410.

Parasuraman, R., R. Molloy, and I. Singh. 2009. "Performance Consequences of Automation-Induced 'Complacency.'" *The International Journal of Aviation Psychology* 19: 1–23.

Roberts, K. H., R. Bea, and D. L. Bartles. 2001. "Must Accidents Happen? Lessons from High Reliability Organizations." *The Academy of Management Executive* 15(3): 70–79.

Stenzel, J. 2010. "Freedom with Fences: Robert Stephens Discusses CIO Leadership and IT Innovation." In: *CIO Best Practices: Enabling Strategic Value with Information Technology*, edited by J. Stenzel 1–23 Cary: SAS Institute Inc.

CHAPTER SIX

The art of containing

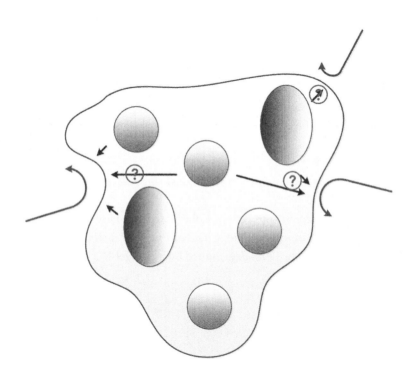

CONTENTS

Your project is prepared and equipped with the necessary flexibility to engage with uncertainty and complexity. The next step is to develop a commitment to contain uncertainty appropriately and to prevent complexity from cascading into a full-blown crisis. Each part of the project must be ready to work together coherently to align the execution of responses with the problems at hand as and when they arise.

Nevertheless, some sub-units in your project will need support to counter each problem mindfully. They cannot always act on their own. Collective ownership goes hand-in-hand with collective accountability, yet this also needs to work in tandem with individual responsibility to act on uncertainties. It is a delicate balance.

THE LURE OF CONTROL

The preparation for your project is done. Not only is the project prepared for the expected, aleatoric uncertainty (risk), but also the unexpected (epistemic uncertainty). The project is in a state of alertness, with participants constantly on the lookout for what might go wrong. Their preparedness goes beyond what one normally expects;

their readiness to act quickly offers a timely resolution before issues can cascade into a crisis. As with all actions, there are behavioural obstacles that may make this state of readiness less effective.

ILLUSION OF CONTROL

The illusion of control is a cognitive bias that leads us to feel we have complete control over a situational outcome where, in fact, we do not. The phenomenon was identified in the 1970s (Langer 1975, 311) as *an expectancy of a personal success probability inappropriately higher than the objective probability would warrant*. What this means is that people feel they can influence outcomes of a particular course of action even when the ability to influence those outcomes may lie partially or wholly in the control of others. More precisely, the illusion of control is connected closely with the use of power. People believe that the unilateral use of power to make changes is the equivalent of control, although this is not necessarily the case (Dermer and Lucas 1986). This is because power can over-inflate peoples' self-esteem to such an extent that they believe they have control, even over uncontrollable situations. This cognitive bias is found to be even more pronounced where people have power thrust upon them or a sudden increase in power, and where they have a high level of familiarity with the situation (Fast et al. 2009).

The effect of the illusion of control can be seen in everyday life. People carrying special talismans or 'lucky tokens' often do so as a means of providing physical evidence that they can channel luck to stay on their side. As with all cognitive biases, there are benefits and drawbacks to this. The illusion of control means that people feel that they are not subject to the vagaries of fate and have some influence over their lives. The drawbacks of unwarranted and excessive illusions of control include unfounded fears and paranoia and delusions that they are either in complete control over events or that events have conspired to defeat them.

A good example of the illusion of control is when people are driving. If they are a passenger, they feel they are more likely to be involved in an accident than if they are driving because, as a passenger, they are out of control, whereas if they are driving they feel in control.

In organisations, the illusion of control can manifest itself in all sorts of ways. For example, although senior management may have a vision for their organisation this is, at best, only partially followed throughout the organisation as a whole. This is because, in many organisations, a single, global vision for the organisation is not implementable but instead becomes a kind of composite vision with the emergence of other modes of control (Pettigrew 1973). In this situation, senior management may believe they have control, but much of this belief is illusory. Another example of the illusion of control at play is in the attempts of management to implement change. While many managers labour under the belief that change can be planned and directed, many researchers have found that much of change is an emergent phenomenon (Dermer and Lucas 1986). Perhaps the most problematic thing about this is that people feel they are to blame when things do not turn out as envisaged, not recognising that their actual control over the situation was partial at best.

HABITUAL RESPONSES

Faced with the challenge of epistemic uncertainty, the temptation for us project managers is to fall back on 'tried and tested' routines and rely on these until it is, perhaps, too late. Where no problems emerge, this behaviour is fine. It is when things start to go awry that reflexively following routines, that have been used successfully before, can become a problem. Indeed, it may be that responses to problems are habitual: if something goes wrong, then certain routines are followed, regardless of the context or nature of the problem. Of course, the main problem with habitual responses is that they are the antithesis of mindful project management. They are an attempt to find a ready-made answer to any problem when in practice these new difficulties often require more innovative and imaginative solutions.

HIERARCHICAL ESCALATION

Where managers encounter uncertainty, there is often a tendency to ask someone more senior to take the crucial decision on how to respond. Frequently, this is not about what action should be taken, but more about passing accountability for decision-making up the hierarchy. This is not always a problem, and it is frequently necessary where there are crucial decisions to be made which may lie outside the control or scope of the project manager (for example, resource allocation across a portfolio of projects). However, the process of escalation can present major problems. This is because escalation of decision-making is slow – it requires the project manager to articulate and communicate the problem clearly to senior management, for people at a more senior level to understand the nature and implications of the problem and then for a decision to be made and communicated. Managers at a more senior level are generally more remote and removed from the project situation and may therefore not be best placed to make decisions. In the time it takes to make a decision, the risky circumstances may well have escalated into something far more problematic for the project, and this could have been avoided if the people closest to the problem had dealt with it straight away. Other, slightly subtler issues arise, too. If a reporting and escalation culture takes root, then any problems or deviations from a plan can result in excessive reporting (for example, daily conference calls being set up), resulting in extensive effort to measure and report rather than actually to fix the problem. This can be painful, and may well cause managers to 'hide' small problems until they can resolve them themselves to avoid extra scrutiny. The upshot of this, of course, is that the first senior management hears of these problems is when they have become full-blown crises that can no longer be concealed.

The problem of inappropriate escalation generally lies in a lack of empowerment on the part of those working where problems are occurring. If they feel unable or unwilling to be accountable for their actions, they will defer decisions rather than take action when it is needed. In mindful project management, escalations are to be avoided. We must 'own' the problem until it is resolved.

PROBLEM OF ACCOUNTABILITY

We may use accountability as a judge instead of a witness; a whipping stick instead of a ruler. That is when accountability becomes a problem. The tendency to avoid this whipping stick escalate problems away, through the organisational hierarchy.

Where there is a lack of empowerment in the project team, decisions will be deferred or escalated. This results in a delay in decision-making and, in turn, allows risks to escalate. The problem lies with us retreating to compliance. If we have 'ticked the box', our job is secure. Compliance becomes a tool for protecting individuals rather than serving the best interests of the project. This goes to the heart of project governance: what does the governance approach seek to achieve? Is it there to blame and castigate individuals for mistakes, or to help the project team achieve objectives? If, where mistakes are made or uncertainty emerges, a scapegoat is sought, no one will want to be accountable for their actions. This puts the whole project at risk.

STATUS QUO BIAS

First formally identified in the 1980s, status quo bias is a prevalent cognitive bias where people prefer their environment and situation to remain as it is (Samuelson and Zeckhauser 1988). Closely related to the concept of inertia (Madrian and Shea 2001), where the stability of prevailing systems often results from status quo bias, this bias affects all sorts of decision-making, from relatively small, low-risk decisions to very significant choices.

As with other cognitive biases, status quo bias affects all people in all walks of life. For example, it has been found that there is great inertia in the UK to changing domestic energy suppliers, despite the process being made incredibly simple and with virtually zero cost with direct monetary savings being available as a result. This can, in part, be explained by status quo bias. Many organisations, such as insurance companies and banks, factor status quo bias into their business models in the expectation that people will not bother to switch accounts, even when offered a more enticing deal.

The psychology of status quo bias closely relates to both cognitive misconceptions (that underpin most cognitive biases) but, in the case of status quo bias, also psychological commitments – people feel committed to a particular situation and, therefore, are reluctant to change. In particular, it is connected with loss aversion, where people weigh the possibility of a loss more highly than they do the possibility of equal amounts of gain, and sunk cost fallacy, where people continue to invest resources into a particular endeavour, even when that endeavour is not beneficial (both these cognitive biases are discussed elsewhere in this book). Status quo bias is also influenced by the mere exposure effect where people prefer something they have been exposed to before.

CONFIRMATION BIAS

First identified in the 1960s (Wason 1960), confirmation bias (sometimes referred to as confirmatory bias) is a cognitive bias that describes the tendency of people to favour new information that confirms their previously held beliefs. Indeed, it has been found that people will actively seek and interpret information that supports their preconceptions. As such, it represents an error of inductive inference towards confirmation of a position held, hypotheses or other pre-existing viewpoints (Nickerson 1998).

Features of confirmation bias are:

- In developing opinions, people look for positive and resist negative cases.
- People need less evidence to form a hypothesis than they need to reject a hypothesis.
- People see what they are looking for, even when it is not there.
- People perceive a higher correlation in data that supports their beliefs than is there.
- People tend to believe things that are desirable to their current way of life. This is closely associated with the status-quo effect and is sometimes called the Pollyanna principle.
- The more strongly people hold a belief, the more likely they will be to confirmation bias.
- People tend to stand by first impressions, even if future information undermines those impressions (Nickerson 1998).

Within organisations, confirmation bias has a profound influence on decision-making. Because people are more concerned about being right than about being wrong, so they find data and information to support their sometimes erroneous views (Chambers and Windschitl 2004). Some of the effects include assuming opinions are factual. Although past performance is not an indicator of future performance, senior managers tend to assume that because organisations have done well in the past, they will do well in the future. People in organisations tend to over-value the way things were done in the past, and confirmation bias reinforces this (Nickerson 1998).

ISOLATION

Just as we tend to look at problems in isolation from the wider picture, we also tend to do this with responses. Responses are defined to match particular uncertainties. However, individual responses can have wider implications beyond the prevention and mitigation of isolated uncertainties. We respond and then move on to the next problem, not necessarily making linkages between them, or appreciating that containment may well trigger new uncertainties, not only for our project but possibly beyond it as well.

NON-COMMITMENT

Uncertainty represents fiction until it materialises. Why act on fiction if all that it does is close off opportunities to act? We may well know about a particular uncertainty but resist commitment, hoping that uncertainty will not materialise, possibly until it is too late. We tend to cling to inaction for two reasons. First, we seek to retain our freedom to act. Second, we seek to avoid commitment of resources that may not be needed. Indeed, when budgets are tight, expenditure on seemingly 'non-essential' activities might lead to awkward questions, so this logic has some rational basis. We believe uncertainty might happen, but hope it will not.

LACK OF REFLECTION

We all like to believe that our decisions are well founded and that we have identified the most effective solutions to uncertainty. However, responses can often be initiated without recourse to scrutiny: to identify whether the chosen response matches the problem at hand and to ensure that our judgement is as good as it could be. This automatism is fuelled by the lack of time for useful reflection. Signs of stress and a full workload are good indicators of a lack of reflection in matching a response to a problem, and this is worth looking out for in both ourselves and our teams.

SUNK-COST FALLACY

Closely related to loss aversion and status quo bias, the sunk-cost fallacy refers to the tendency of people to continue to pursue a particular endeavour or behaviour as a result of previously invested resources. Those resources need not just be capital but could also take the form of time or effort (Arkes and Blumer 1985). The misconception behind this tendency is that people think they are making rational decisions based on the future value of their investments whereas, in truth, their decisions are tainted by investments they have already made, to which they have an emotional attachment. This emotional attachment becomes more difficult to break, the more the investment accumulates.

Sunk-cost is a fallacy because it prevents people from taking the best course of action. People become wedded to a specific course, even when it is detrimental to them simply because they have a large, and often increasing, stake in the action.

Psychologists have found that the sunk-cost fallacy affects all aspects of life. It results in people staying with partners who are inappropriate or problematic for their health and well-being. Gamblers chase losses, people overspend on products for which they have no need and consume products and services even when the cost of doing so outweighs the benefits (Sweis et al. 2018).

In organisations, the sunk-cost fallacy leads to people committing to investments and pouring more and more resources into those investments when, often, the wisest course of action is to cut one's losses. The result is that people in organisations are prepared to throw good money after bad (Arkes and Blumer 1985).

KEY ENABLERS TO THE ART OF CONTAINING

One thing that *is* certain about uncertainty is that it is likely to emerge at some point during a project. Uncertainty can take many forms and often threatens to derail projects in terms of both timescale and budget, and it may well jeopardise the realisation of long-term benefits. It is our job to contain uncertainty through adaptation and through continuous commitment to the management of uncertainty.

COMMITMENT

To foster resilience, people in projects need to work together in multidisciplinary teams. This means removing remove barriers to cross-functional collaboration. From a resilience standpoint, encouraging mindful thinking in team members to accommodate epistemic uncertainty is crucial and requires a commitment. This means breaking the tendency to operate mindlessly compliant to a project management framework.

Commitment is the social 'glue' in a project and can be a compelling reason to focus on project delivery. In resilient projects, commitment is not just restricted to our work – we commit to our relationships, friendships; the causes we 'truly' care about.

Ensuring team commitment is not just an act of leadership at the moment though; it needs to be built up over time so that the project or organisational culture is one of dedication to the work and personal commitment to project objectives. This is neither straightforward nor without cost but, when potential crises are successfully averted, this effort will seem like a price well worth paying.

ABUNDANT EXPERTISE

Expertise is not to be confused with 'experts'. Expertise (proficiency, skill, specialist knowledge) is not a permanent state of being but is situational, based on current needs and previous experiences. Expertise is also relational in that it is an assemblage of knowledge, experience, learning and intuition that is seldom embodied in just a single individual.

An expert is often defined as someone very knowledgeable in a particular area. Expertise is unlikely to be defined by hierarchy, status or ego. Nor is it necessarily asserted through accreditations, as these can be just forms of knowledge-testing. 'True' expertise combines deep factual knowledge in a particular field and a way of appreciating that it is dynamic. There is rarely only 'one best way' of doing things in a complex situation and solutions and choices are likely to evolve. The expert's opinion is not to be mistaken for the end of a discussion about an answer. Instead, expertise is the beginning of a discourse, triggering a process of fact-finding, knowledge-generation and problem-solving.

SENSITIVITY

Any response based on expertise not only has an immediate impact on the problem – hopefully for the better – but may have consequences for other projects, units or departments of the organisation as a whole. Just imagine that you have responded to uncertainty through taking actions to reduce the likelihood of its occurrence or to mitigate its impact. This is generally a positive process since uncertainty is being actively addressed, as it should be. However, it is important also to keep in mind and be sensitive to the impact on the wider environment. The big picture goes beyond the problem and solution at hand. It looks beyond the task or even the project boundaries and incorporates a wider perspective; that of a programme or even a business in which the project is embedded. Management not only involves zooming 'in' to the management of tasks but also zooming 'up and out' to see how project work relates to the bigger picture. A big picture approach looks at the wider impact of decisions and needs a broad appreciation of goals, priorities and work methods if we are to be able to make sensible judgements in the light of the effects our decisions may have.

IMPROVISATION

In resilient projects, we understand the importance of routines and procedures for predictable behaviour in delivering the work, but we also know that none of us has perfect knowledge about how to respond to epistemic uncertainty. The unexpected is inevitable. With these surprises comes the necessity to improvise – the need for staff to think on their feet. Knowledgeable project teams need to have the freedom and space to self-organise into *ad hoc* networks to provide expert problem-solving. These networks have no formal status and dissolve as soon as a crisis is over.

Weick (1998, 552) provides a list of characteristics of teams that are required to be highly capable of improvising:

- Willingness to forego planning and to rehearse in favour of acting in real-time.
- Well-developed understanding of internal resources and the materials that are at hand.
- Proficiency without blueprints and diagnosis.
- Ability to identify or agree on minimal structures for embellishing.
- Openness to reassembly of and departures from routines.
- Possession of a rich and meaningful set of themes, fragments or phrases on which to draw for ongoing lines of action.
- Predisposition to recognise the partial relevance of previous experience to present novelty.
- High confidence in the team's skill to deal with non-routine events.
- The availability of associates committed to and competent at impromptu making do.
- Skill in paying attention to the performance of others and building on it to keep the interaction going and to set up interesting possibilities for one another.
- Ability to match and maintain the pace and tempo at which others are extemporising.
- Focus on coordination here and now without being distracted by memories or anticipation.
- Preference for and comfort with process rather than structure, which makes it easier to work with ongoing development, restructuring and realisation of outcomes, and easier to postpone the question, 'what will it have amounted to?'

MINDFUL PRACTICES
SPONTANEITY THROUGH IMPROVISATION

Being at the forefront of technology has the dual benefit of providing interest and engagement for employees while enabling the company to spot new business opportunities. TTP has created new groups and formed several spinoff companies as such opportunities were identified. In exploring, adapting to clients' needs and spotting new opportunities, management has found that:

> One of the key messages that we have here is to be prepared to improvise.

Project managers in TTP face challenges that require new, spontaneous responses. This is because, at times where planning and execution converge, quick actions are necessary. The work that is required in an environment of pressure and uncertainty becomes less 'formalised' and more improvisational:

> People generally have the instinct to try to do things 'properly'; you see it incorporate 'strategy and things like that where 'here's the target' – I know our big clients do this – here's the target, how do we marshal everything to get there?' Actually, in a creative entrepreneurial environment – and you can do it if you are a smaller organisation – it's more about what are the opportunities, what's in front of us and how do we improvise, from that? Darwin, actually as well as the adaptability thing, mentioned improvisation in terms of successful species. It is a central topic, and I think it's one that's missed in general, not just risk but in business generally.

Key to improvisational working is, first and foremost, an acknowledgement that improvisation is not a sign of 'bad planning'. Indeed, improvisation works best in a culture in which processes and plans can be circumvented, albeit with set boundaries. Such deviations from 'planned activities' are supported at TTP. Scrutiny is not limited by compliance thinking, improvisational capabilities are not fostered by compliance audits. Instead, the power of improvisation is measured by its creativity and adaptability. The question of consistency of action is replaced by the question of whether the 'right' action has been carried out in a timely fashion.

Going hand-in-hand with empowerment (letting go), improvisation (making do) leads to increased creative outcomes that are novel and yet at times appear not to be useful. The outcome of improvisational activities might lead to otherwise 'wasteful' activities such as 'near-misses'. However, in the culture of TTP, such near-misses are seen as opportunities – opportunities to learn.

Improvisation can be prepared for. TTP does not just leave its project managers to 'do their own thing'. Improvisational capabilities are pre-established through training. Again, it is important to point out that compliance to management frameworks – what one should do – is not high on TTP's training agenda. Rather, the aim is to provide project managers with an understanding of what empowerment and improvisation entail – what one can do – to deal with situations that are characterised by urgency and uncertainty.

What is mindful about it? The word improvisation stems from the Latin word 'improvisus'. In essence, it implies the thinking and acting in the 'here' and 'now' in the absence of being prepared for or having planned for a situation. We may become absorbed in the moment, and advocate self-censorship in believing we can simply rely on a pre-loaded, past-informed action.

Traditional project management framework, with an emphasis on deterministic and probabilistic planning, may enable us to work just right to the edges of the risk horizon. Beyond it, we can not rely on pre-determined instruction but have to engage with a discomforting experience of improvising.

Improvisation is a powerful skill that adds to resilience. It can be developed and fostered but also needs to be supported by a culture of trust, respect and mutual support. Improvisational skills enable us to be prepared for epistemic uncertainty that are truly unexpected but require swift action.

FREEDOM TO THINK

Improvisation is not carried out in a vacuum. Any action, as novel as it might be, needs to be synchronous – as in a jazz band – with the 'tunes' of other players, namely the other stakeholders. Our freedom to think and act requires alignment and commitment to the success of the collective (not just their individual success). Thinking about how and why one should respond is paramount, but requires time. Such time is often scarce. We tend to be preoccupied with the 'how' – doing things according to what has been pre-planned – and less so with a reflection on responses and their alignment to the bigger picture.

LEADING THE ART OF CONTAINING

Where time is sufficient to prevent a crisis from happening, leadership is required to support the containment of uncertainty. It is tempting to pre-load responses and make people do what has been defined in advance. Uncertainty makes such an approach in itself risky, as novelty and ambiguity require reflection and deliberation, not necessarily the 'blind', almost 'unthinking' adherence to what has been defined as a response to a past problem.

INCREASING READINESS

Preparation is just part of the story, though. The preparation of us and key stakeholders means that we have the organisational system and understanding in place to scan for and communicate uncertainty and that we are not complacent about our preparedness. However, readiness implies that our team is set to put its preparation into action, to be willing to execute what one has prepared for.

Such commitment to act immediately – when adversity strikes – requires a number of other factors. Key among these is transparency. People must be encouraged not to conceal or hide problems, and the outcomes of projects should be measured using an agreed methodology. Apart from anything else, public reporting of outcomes can act as a powerful driver for improvement.

It is also crucial to link everybody's behaviour to the desired outcomes. If we want others to be committed to resilience, they need to be rewarded for this kind of behaviour. This might include the following:

- Bonuses can be linked to behaviour-based expectations (BBEs). Originally used in the nuclear power industry, BBEs are typically agreed among employee peers, and they hold each other accountable for seeing that they are fulfilled. They are designed to tackle some common causes of failure, such as lack of attention to detail, lack of critical thinking, noncompliance with policies and behaviours in high-risk situations. They generally involve ensuring that simple tasks are performed accurately every time, perhaps by developing mnemonics (for checklists) when people are performing repetitive tasks.
- Ensuring that individual owners are identified for all actions, rather than having responses owned by the team. This way, actions are more likely to be implemented.
- Where expected behaviours are exhibited, advancement opportunities are made available.

FACILITATING IMPROVISATION

Improvisation can take on a purposeful, considered dimension. A commitment to resilience in projects requires an expectation that project teams will improvise around unexpected problems. In this context, improvisation is not a complete absence of structure in decision-making, implying chaos, randomness, and disorder. It is not simply 'making it up as you go along'. Using jazz as a metaphor, the performers – us, as project staff – improvise around a structure and plan. Like jazz musicians, improvising managers continuously invent novel responses without a predetermined script and with little certainty as to the exact outcomes of their actions. The consequences of their decisions unfold as the activities themselves are enacted.

Key to this process is an activity termed 'provocative competence', where managers instigate a departure from routines and 'recipe' behaviours, treating errors as a source of learning. They can alternate between 'soloing' and 'supporting' to give the team room to think, enhance learning and distribute the leadership task. There are five steps to provocative competence:

1. The affirmative move, where the manager has an excellent knowledge of the team's capabilities, often understanding individual team members' strengths better than they do themselves.
2. Introduction of a small disruption to the routine, such as shifting a regular meeting to a different location or time, or switching personnel around.
3. Giving the team a stretch-assignment to solve.
4. Facilitating incremental reorientation by encouraging repetition. This involves learning new routines or ways of doing things based on the problems they have solved.
5. Analogic sharpening – the provocative competence intervention should allow the team to work out new links and connections that they can employ in problem-solving. This might, for example, be new or better understanding of other peoples' skills, or new knowledge about resources that they could call upon when faced with a crisis.

CREATING 'SPACE' TO REFLECT

Any response exercised in a project needs to be reflected upon, as the problem at hand might have changed in the meantime. However, we also need to keep project momentum going to meet the inevitably tight deadlines. We need to create space for ourselves, to think about the 'why'. Why did we do this? What was the purpose of this response and has it had the desired effect? These are just some of the questions that need to be addressed repeatedly. Private, personal reflection is powerful and short daily meetings can also be used to gain greater insight. A suggested balance between 'doing' and 'reflecting' is 90/10. Given the intensity of most projects, this is likely to be challenging. However, it is a powerful approach since it is foolish to believe that a future will unfold exactly as planned. Time spent slowing down is likely to be time well spent on reflection.

DEFERRING TO EXPERTISE

As mentioned before, improvisation is not chaos. It is a state of highly situated thinking, dealing with problems in the here-and-now. Such thinking in a collective – as a project normally is – requires expertise both to challenge and also to supplement one another. The hierarchies of traditional, stable project teams can be too inflexible and slow to see and respond to uncertainty in a prompt and effective manner. By the time 'permission' to act has been escalated up the hierarchy to a higher authority, the problem in question may already have spun out of control. This is because there is, understandably, a premium placed on progress in projects. The project schedule is one of the key objectives of the work and progress is frequently valued as a key priority. The idea of stopping the project is an anathema to many managers. However, where a problem is identified early, work could be paused briefly to deal with the problem effectively before it becomes much more significant. Caught early, the issue is likely to be relatively small in scope and scale and isolated to a particular part of the project system. The team has to deal with it in a focused manner and then it can move on.

This then brings us to a key principle for containing adversity in resilient projects – deference to expertise. Resilient projects push decision-making 'down and around'. Those who are close to uncertainty are often best-placed to deal with the problem. They should not be 'left on their own' to make the best decisions, though. As we have already observed, people in resilient projects are empowered beyond their expertise. However, we must support them with expertise, to enable both us and others we have empowered to take action, to make the most informed judgement.

Expertise, residing in the project and beyond, needs to be made transparent to us 'owning' the management of uncertainty. We need to be made aware of these informal networks, and such expertise needs to be made readily available to us to inform our decision-making.

AUTHORITY BIAS

Sometimes called obedience bias, authority bias is a cognitive bias describing the tendency of people to attribute greater weight and accuracy to the opinions of authority figures. This is found to happen even when people believe what those in authority are saying, or how they are behaving, is wrong. People are likely to value the opinions of those in authority over their own.

Blind obedience to authority was revealed in the infamous Milgram Shock experiment in the early 1960s in which participants believed they were administering increasingly harmful shocks to an unseen participant. Despite their misgivings, about two-thirds of the participants in the experiment were prepared to continue increasing the electric shocks to a fatal level under the instruction of an authority figure (in this case, a man in a laboratory coat) (Smith and Bond 1998).

Authority bias is, in fact, an important aspect of everyday life, driven by a deep-seated duty to authority among people. Police and judicial members rely on this, as do medical and educational staff. For example, people generally follow medical advice based on the authority of the medical practitioner. This is the case for anyone, including other people in authority. This effect has been seen to extend to people who are listened to, such as social media influencers.

However, while deference to authority is useful as a kind of social glue, it also has problems. In organisations, people can sometimes do as they are instructed mindlessly, rather than questioning their instruction. This means that organisations might participate in ethically suspect actions at the behest of senior management even despite the misgivings of staff. Similarly, the ideas and innovations of senior management might be seen as superior to those of other people in the organisation, even when they are in fact inferior, simply because of the authority of the proposer.

Resilient projects have mastered the ability to alter their typical patterns of containing adversity – they allow the situated voices to be heard. In practice, for resilient project organisations, this means:

- All project workers are valued, and expertise is seen as an asset.
- Everyone must be comfortable sharing information and concerns with anyone at any time.
- Project managers defer to the person with the most knowledge of the issue at hand.
- Everyone works together to find the best solution.

Our role as a project leader is not to be that single expert or to assume that those close to uncertainty have all the necessary expertise that comes with empowerment. Expertise needs to be identified and made accessible. People need to be made aware of pockets of expertise and how to access them, without great bureaucratic hurdles.

We need to encourage a culture in which expertise is acknowledged, cherished, and rewarded. This can take many forms. For example, morning briefings can reinforce deference to expertise using conversational methods, such as non-verbal cues (eye contact, gestures), making problems immediate to people's situations rather than repeating redundant information, and the use of engaging descriptions and storytelling techniques. Whatever method (or a mix of methods) is used, it should be rich, current, and relevant to the needs of the project workers at that moment. The key is to provoke a conversation around expertise beyond 'surface' information and to spread this knowledge through the interpersonal – and often informal – networks involved in the project. Developing deference to expertise is less about training and more about changing processes. The first step is to redefine meetings. The best place for conversations is in the work area – not in conference rooms or formal meetings. We can adopt 'no-meeting time zones' so managers can circulate the project space and receive feedback from other project workers. By observing progress and meeting with employees in their actual workspace, we can more easily defer to employees' expertise and customs.

DEALING WITH THE ACCOUNTABILITY PROBLEM

Problems are 'owned' by the person closest to them until they can either resolve them or find someone else who can. In resilient projects, problem-based decisions should be taken by those best placed to do so. The challenge in this is that people who experience a great deal of accountability tend to make more appropriate decisions, but sometimes intense accountability can only be relieved by ratcheting decisions up the organisational hierarchy. This is more likely in circumstances where political pressure and career concerns are great.

Hence, we should not confuse accountability as a judgment of our inability to be that fail-safe able to predict the future state of a project and prevent all uncertainty from impacting the project. Accountability can not, and must not, be associated with the inability to prevent something uncertain from materialising; accountability may well relate to not 'owning' uncertainty or negligence but mindfully engaging with it.

SUPPORTING 'JUST' CONTAINMENT

The principles underpinning responsiveness in containing uncertainty raise some issues. Perhaps the most profound is that of culture. A resilient project needs a culture that supports the mindful behaviours demanded of the project team. Resilient projects are imbued with what is called a 'just' culture. The key focus of this kind of cultural milieu is to concentrate on what is wrong (with the system) rather than on who is at fault. Even one small pocket of failure that is missed could ultimately threaten to derail the project. If we think we will be blamed for the problem, or that the default response will be to identify someone who is at fault, then the early, weak signals will go unreported and mindful engagement with uncertainty will slacken. The types of problems and appropriate responses can be seen below (see Table 6.1):

Table 6.1 *Just behaviour*

Mechanism of duty breach	Appropriate response
Human error: this is an inadvertent slip, lapse, or mistake.	Console the individual. Improve and failure-proof the system that allowed the breach.
At-risk behaviour: this is a conscious drift from resilient behaviour, occurring when an individual believes that drift doesn't cause harm.	Assess the system for weaknesses that encourage or require the individual to take risks. Improve and failure-proof the system that allowed the breach. Coach the individual; take disciplinary action on repeated risky behaviour.
Reckless behaviour: the individual consciously chooses to engage in behaviour that has unjustified and substantial risk.	Determine if the individual is impaired or unwilling to follow standard work principles. Discipline or provide employee assistance as appropriate.

Marx (2009)

MINDFUL PRACTICES
A 'JUST' CULTURE

At TTP, there is a need to learn from errors and mistakes. Mishaps, close calls and process upsets are sources from which one can draw lessons:

We expect that people will make mistakes ... the task of the more senior guys is to manage the consequences of a junior making mistakes. If you're not allowed to make any mistakes, sooner or later you will, and they'll be big ones.

Dealing with mistakes can be seen as an acknowledgement of failure, and thus incompetence. Why did the project manager not do the right thing in the first place? It is therefore tempting to ignore mistakes and not share them with others. However, only a small proportion of errors are the result of incompetence or malicious behaviour – something that might justify some blame and penalty. TTP takes active steps to avoid a 'culture of blame' that would undermine the emphasis on teams. There is

> *very little blame internally ... the people who stay awake all night worrying, they will beat themselves up, they do not need to have somebody else telling them that they have done a bad job.*

A 'just' culture is not to be mistaken for a 'no-blame' culture, which is neither feasible nor desirable. A blanket amnesty, the core of a 'no-blame' culture, without any sanctions opens the floodgates for unacceptable behaviour. Instead, a 'just' culture provides the encouragement to project leaders at TTP to report and share 'honest' mistakes with internal and external stakeholders. This allows a quick resolution and also facilitates information exchange as a prerequisite for reflection and learning.

Understandably, people are reluctant to share incidents that are burdened with the connotation of failure. As a consequence, TTP emphasises two main issues – confidentiality and fairness. Incidents of errors are communicated without the allocation of blame, and people are incentivised, and occasionally rewarded, for speaking honestly about mistakes and errors in projects they were responsible for. Sanctions for unacceptable behaviours are openly communicated so that people can draw a line against what 'just' implies. It is of great importance that people at TTP are treated fairly. Hence the response to an incident is often explained and justified, to allow people to understand the 'why', without bias and the feeling of injustice.

What is mindful about it? A just culture holds us responsible for the quality of our choice and actions. It provides us with the freedom to act, allows us to improvise within boundaries. In a just culture, we are not only made accountable for our own actions, but also accountable to each other. It is important to note that the onus does not lie on the outcome but on the process. If, for example, we have done our utmost to contain uncertainty, but due to aspects outside of our control project performance deteriorates, we as project managers need to feel 'safe enough' to improvise. Only under conditions of gross-negligence should penalties and punishments be imposed.

SUPPORTING MINDFUL CONTAINMENT

As we mentioned earlier, in a resilient project, the person who responds to a problem – because they are closest to it and thus most familiar with it – is generally to be supported in making the most informed judgement. However, in drawing on his or her specific expertise, the individual may look at the problem in isolation from the larger view of what that problem could mean for the project and the wider business. We may well execute a response without thinking about the potential consequences of it on the big picture (see Figure 6.1).

Hence, we need to make sure that we are sensitive to what that big picture includes and challenge them to make the connection between their response and its possible wider consequences. The simple question 'What does this mean for … ?' may suffice to kick-start this consequential thinking. Widening someone's appreciation will also influence their ownership. Something that, looked at in isolation, may appear to be relatively inconsequential, might suddenly become more important if seen in the context of the bigger picture.

We need to have good oversight and be aware of the wider implications of responses to uncertainty, rather than becoming embroiled in the

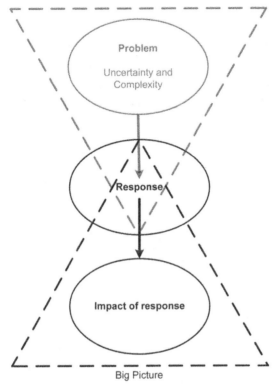

Figure 6.1 *Big picture thinking – solution*

detail. Yes, we are formally project managers but, in our leadership role, getting involved in day-to-day issues may divert attention from the broader, system-wide issues. Keeping sight of the big picture means that we will be able to help the project team form and maintain a shared sense of the adversities it faces and the appropriate actions to take.

THE IMPACT OF CONTAINING ON RELATIONSHIPS

The containment of uncertainty is driven by a continuous engagement with stakeholders to help contain that uncertainty. Such promises to mindfully engage with uncertainty may erode in the light of adverse effects of uncertainty, and thus need to be reinforced.

ASSESSING CONTRIBUTION

The first task for us is to assess the actual contribution of stakeholders to the management of uncertainty. This may start with an assessment of how tolerant stakeholders are in light of emerging uncertainty. Do they see materialising uncertainty as a natural evolution or indeed something that is perceived as inadequate planning? The latter may drive an attribution of blame that is destructive to the continuous commitment of stakeholders to keep on managing uncertainty in a collaborative manner. In this respect, it is important to pick up signals of a deteriorating relationship.

DRIVING COMMITMENT OF STAKEHOLDERS

How can we engage stakeholders in the process of, in the extreme, constant improvisation? Against all odds, we have to anticipate what is coming next before it happens. In other words, what is required is a heightened state of mind, an awareness, playful engagement and the flow of improvisation. Maintaining such a playful improv engagement with uncertainty needs to be nurtured through collaboration and inspiration. One key driver of mental stimulation is to appeal to individual dedication towards the group that are relied upon to deliver the project. As a project is essentially a social undertaking, people need to be inspired and socially committed to act in the best interest of people, aligned with the objectives of the project.

MINDFUL PRACTICES
ORGANISATIONAL IDENTIFICATION AND BELONGING

How individuals determine value for themselves is a deciding factor in choosing to join an organisation or project. The extent to which members commit to something as temporary as a project is very much dependent on the value of belonging and on identifying one's values with those of the project and the organisation. The sense of belonging at TTP is driven by the creation of personal relationships. It is:

> one of the most powerful things. People will join resources from the other groups, and they make a personal bond.

After-work social groups, sports teams, and working on community issues all help foster a sense of shared purpose including,

> *the fact that they eat in the same restaurant, that sort of social mixing.*

Social bonding is also encouraged within TTP. This can be in the form of providing support and peer reviews to other project leaders, or by honestly sharing stories of project successes and failures. The purpose is to create the identity of a project manager who is both professional and committed. For TTP, a professional manager is one who possesses a wide range of knowledge and has gained extensive experience. They have the skills to manage a project successfully. These skills need to be channelled towards a purpose, and to forming a 'bridge' – a bond – with other people in the organisation. This includes a strong understanding of what the organisation and project stand for. The value of a sense of belonging should not be underestimated.

What is mindful about it? A cohesive team is one that bonds; meaning that we pick up the slack of others while working towards a shared goal. Fundamental to a socially cohesive project team is the capacity to experience a heightened state of mindfulness about epistemic uncertainty, in a group. This includes the ability to appreciate conflicting perspectives, the 'safe space' to challenge and question each other for the purpose to instil curiosity, creativity and engagement beyond the realm of the risk horizon. In other words, social cohesion is the foundation of mindful management of epistemic uncertainty.

ADDRESSING THE ACCOUNTABILITY PROBLEM

We have talked about the importance of accountability and the establishment of a 'just culture'. We have also explored the role of culture in supporting accountability and both facilitating and controlling empowerment. Therefore, it is incumbent on us to see that the project develops its own culture that de-emphasises accountability as a means of attributing blame but, rather, inspires dedication in stakeholders to do their best to contain uncertainty. This process may be reinforced by implementing policies that support just culture and translating a just culture into mindful project practices and processes.

NEVER-ENDING COMMITMENT TO CONTAINMENT

It must be acknowledged that containing adversity is an ongoing process and not a one-off activity. Uncertainty constantly jeopardises project performance. By no means can adversity be fully prevented from materialising. Indeed, it can only be subdued to the extent that variation in project performance may remain within acceptable tolerances. Hence, all the parties involved need to acknowledge that the initial 'ideal' of project performance may never be achieved.

BELL BOEING V-22 OSPREY – A SUCCESS OF CONTAINING?

The previous vignettes all talk about a failure of noticing, interpreting, or preparing for the unexpected in a mindful manner. There is indeed a plethora of case studies of projects struggling to adequately look beyond the risk horizon. However, once the unexpected emerges and can no longer be ignored, projects tend to successfully mobilise activities to contain or recover from a crisis. But, at what cost?

On 8 April 2000, a V-22 Osprey, an American tiltrotor aircraft in development, attempted to land at Marana Northwest Regional Airport as part of a training exercise. Upon approach, it suddenly stalled and crashed, killing 19 Marines. The Osprey earned a terrible reputation during development, costing the lives of 30 Marines in three crashes.

The idea of an aeroplane that could take off vertically like a helicopter and fly horizontally at high speeds and over long distances was realised by the US Military with the program Joint Advanced Vertical Lift Aircraft (JVX), led by Bell Boeing, in 1981.

The programme was plagued with problems from the beginning. The US Army withdraw its commitment in 1987 due to budget constraints, leaving the US Special Ops Command (US SOCOM) to be the sole buyer.

The first of six prototypes made its maiden flight in March 1989. In April 1989, the V-22 programme was cancelled in the 1990 fiscal year's amended budget. Nevertheless, funding and design studies continued, while increasing interest in the Osprey was shown by the US Congress.

The fifth prototype lifted off on 11 June 1991. To observers and the press, this test flight turned out to be a 'rodeo ride'. The Osprey rose into the air, hovered in mid-air, and while trying to land, it violently shrugged to the left and right, until its blades hit the ground and disintegrated. House Representative Dave Weldon committed to the *Deleware County Daily Times*: '*I'd rather it happens now than with Marines on board*' (Whittle 2010, 199).

From July 1992, a string of accidents led to the loss of more Marines. In July 1992, nine Marines died on board of a pre-production V-22. April 2000 saw the biggest loss of life of 19 Marines during a simulation of a rescue exercise. In December 2000, a V-22 got out of control, killing all four aboard.

Despite these tragic setbacks, the developmental testing period showed that the V-22 met or exceeded all performance and handling quality requirements. The combination of speed, range, and vertical takeoff capability has made it unrivalled as a tiltrotor concept.

In projects, trial-and-error (at times at a terrible price) learning is characterised by repeated, varied attempts, which are continued until success is achieved. Surprising problems may then be addressed by improvisational activities that are not directed by pre-loaded action, as there is often no reference in the past or a script that predisposes how to act. The discomfort to address epistemic uncertainty without specific and scripted action is compensated by the commitment to 'try something out'. Rewards and incentives are designed to allow and commit managers to be creative in their containment of uncertainty, much less so to make them mindlessly compliant to pre-loaded actions.

TOWARDS AN ART OF CONTAINING

A resilient project requires dedication and a desire to respond to uncertainty. Such a desire can only be realised if we are empowered and skilled beyond their 'silo' of allocated responsibility and accountability. In this respect, the escalation of decisions up the organisational hierarchy to receive greater authority to enact a response is strongly discouraged.

Empowerment is a crucial component of achieving a commitment to resilience, the confidence in improvising and the ability of us to harness the latent expertise. This expertise can be valuable when directed to dealing with uncertainty in the here-and-now. However, empowerment does not mean that we give up control, as this would be a risk in and of itself. The question becomes one of how we protect their projects from control failures when empowered employees are encouraged to redefine how they go about doing their jobs, improvising and acting autonomously.

Equipping people with range flexibility may allow forms of improvisation. This, though, is not to be mistaken for an acknowledgement of bad planning, since improvisation is a key skill in a project team. However, it can only be applied successfully if the 'big picture' is established and maintained. Responses exercised in isolation of their wider impact are simply a 'shot from the hip' and are potentially dangerous.

Unsurprisingly, we need to support and inspire those around us who happen to be most qualified to contain uncertainty, resisting the temptation to take over. It is our task not to be bogged down in day-to-day work but to provide a support network that allows people closer to the problems and more qualified to deal with them in a timely and appropriate fashion; through inspiration and dedication towards the individual.

Reflection *How well do the following statements characterise your project? For each item, select one box only that best reflects your conclusion.*

	Fully agree		Neither agree nor disagree		Fully disagree
People are committed to engaging with uncertainty.	1	2	3	4	5
Ambiguity in predicting the future is not a hindrance to creating practical responses to it.	1	2	3	4	5
People are empowered beyond their immediate responsibility.	1	2	3	4	5

	Fully agree		Neither agree nor disagree		Fully disagree
Training and expertise are provided to allow people to deal with abnormal situations.	1	2	3	4	5
The big picture is shared, maintained and committed to.	1	2	3	4	5
Hierarchical escalations are an indicator of a lack of empowerment.	1	2	3	4	5

	Fully agree		Neither agree nor disagree		Fully disagree
Expertise is valued more highly than hierarchy, status and position.	1	2	3	4	5
Project leaders help and support in facilitating a response, yet they do not take over if something goes wrong.	1	2	3	4	5
Unless grossly negligent, people are not penalised for enacting a 'wrong' response.	1	2	3	4	5

Scoring: Add the numbers. If you score higher than 27, your capability to contain uncertainty would appear to be good. If you score 27 or lower, please think of how you may be able to enhance your capability to respond to uncertainty appropriately and promptly.

REFERENCES

Arkes, H. R., and C. Blumer. 1985. "The Psychology of Sunk Cost."
Organizational Behavior and Human Decision Processes 35(1): 124–40.

Chambers, J. R., and P. D. Windschitl. 2004. "Biases in Social Comparative
Judgments: The Role of Nonmotivated Factors in above-Average and
Comparative-Optimism Effects." *Psychological Bulletin* 130(5): 813–38.

Dermer, J. D., and R. G. Lucas. 1986. "The Illusion of Managerial Control."
Accounting, Organizations and Society 11(6): 471–82.

Fast, N. J., D. H. Gruenfeld, N. Sivanathan, and A. D. Galinsky. 2009.
"Illusory Control: A Generative Force Behind Power's Far-Reaching Effects."
Psychological Science 20(4): 502–08.

Langer, E. J. 1975. "The Illusion of Control." *Journal of Personality and Social
Psychology* 32(2): 311–28.

Madrian, B. C., and D. F. Shea. 2001. "The Power of Suggestion: Inertia in
401(k) Participation and Savings Behavior." *Quarterly Journal of Economics*
116(4): 1149–87.

Marx, D. 2009. *Whack-a-Mole: The Price We Pay for Expecting*. Plano: By Your
Side Studios.

Nickerson, R. 1998. "Confirmation Bias: A Ubiquitous Phenomenon in Many
Guises." *Review of General Psychology* 2(2): 175–220.

Pettigrew, A. 1973. *The Politics of Organizational Decision Making*. London:
Tavistock.

Samuelson, W., and R. Zeckhauser. 1988. "Status Quo Bias in Decision
Making." *Journal of Risk and Uncertainty* 1(1): 7–59.

Smith, P. B., and M. H. Bond. 1998. *Social Psychology across Cultures*. New
Jersey: Prentice-Hall.

Sweis, B. M., S. V. Abram, B. J. Schmidt, K. D. Seeland, A. W. MacDonald,
M. J. Thomas, and A. David Redish. 2018. "Sensitivity to 'Sunk Costs' in
Mice, Rats, and Humans." *Science* 361(6398): 178–81.

Wason, P. C. 1960. "On the Failure to Eliminate Hypotheses in a Conceptual
Task." *Quarterly Journal of Experimental Psychology* 12(3): 129–40.

Weick, K. E. 1998. "Improvisation as a Mindset for Organizational Analysis."
Organization Science 9(5): 543–55.

Whittle, R. 2010. *The Dream Machine – the Untold History of the Notorious V-22
Osprey*. New York: Simon & Schuster.

CHAPTER SEVEN

The art of recovering

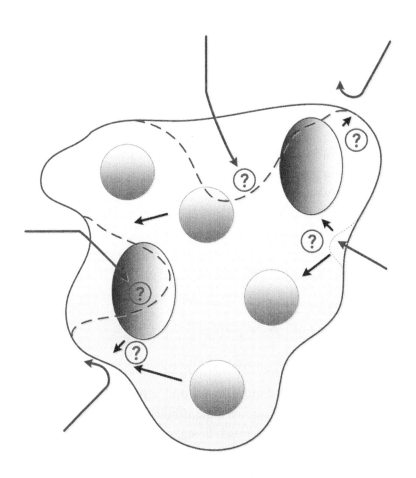

CONTENTS

You may not have been able to prevent all uncertainties from influencing your project; the preceding normality has cascaded into a crisis in which your project's continuation is threatened. Unsurprisingly, this is a time of considerable stress. Yet, it is a time in which clarity is required, and mindless actions need to be avoided. With emotions being stretched to the limit, objectivity is of the utmost importance to enable an appropriate recovery.

THE LURE OF A 'GREAT ESCAPE'

Imagine, that all that has been written in the previous chapters has not worked out. Uncertainty and complexity have taken its toll and if no actions are taken – swiftly – the project might be suspended or stopped altogether. With so much at stake, what do you do? When a crisis hits a project, there are often specific types of behaviours, similar to the ones described in the previous chapters and yet considerably amplified. These, too, are counterproductive because, ironically, they can reinforce the chaos instead of helping with a solution.

THE DEFENSIVE RETREAT

In a crisis characterised by chaos, one is likely to lose orientation: 'Where are we?', 'What is happening?' and 'What shall we do (quickly)?' are some of the questions that we ask ourselves in a crisis. As a result, and because of that uncomfortable feeling of 'being lost', we often tend to fall back on our basic instinct: of self-preservation. We become more inward-looking and try to cover ourselves as individuals. Divisions that emerged during the incubation time (if there was any) may intensify. Instead of more collaboration, we shift towards more adversarial relationships. We start building a wall around us that offers an illusion of comfort. Mindful decision-making becomes less likely.

OSTRICH EFFECT

The term the 'ostrich effect' was coined in the early 2000s (Galai and Sade 2006) to describe the inclination of people to avoid thinking about negative issues in their life, even though those issues might be pressing and need to be dealt with. This behaviour is likened to the myth of ostriches sticking their heads in the sand in the face of extreme danger rather than fleeing (this is a myth: ostriches do not do this but will always try to flee and if they cannot, will flop to the ground and lie prone, ready to escape should the opportunity afford itself). The metaphor of people sticking their 'head in the sand' rather than facing up to problems is not a new one but took a long time to be identified as a specific cognitive bias. From a psychological perspective, it is the result of the tension between what people recognise to be essential and what people anticipate will be painful. The uncomfortable reality does not go away, but people prefer to delude themselves into thinking there is no problem as long as they can, before responding with panic and stress when they are forced to act (Babad and Katz 1991).

What is true of everyday life applies to organisational life as well. For example, in some situations where people are confronted with risks, they may delay responding in the hope things will improve (Kutsch and Hall 2005). Elsewhere, it was found that market traders continually monitored stock performance when markets were performing well but much less frequently when markets were flat or falling, thereby not taking action in time to protect their portfolio values (Karlsson et al. 2009).

BROKEN COMMUNICATION

Going hand-in-hand with increased defensiveness in the face of a crisis is a change in the way we communicate. Communication can be used to preserve our integrity and even to damage others. Information is exchanged, not necessarily to explore what is happening or what we should do next but to lessen any potential blame attaching to oneself. Emails sent for the purpose of explaining one's decisions and leaving a trail to be used later to justify one's actions make sense in that narrow personal context, but may not help the project in the here-and-now. Communication can degenerate into accusations and thus becomes more destructive than helpful in crisis recovery. It is especially important to look for this in inter-departmental or client-provider communication as each group may well retreat to its own domain for relative safety if it seems as if the project is unravelling. When trust falters, resorting to formal communication alone can virtually eliminate the spontaneity, collaboration and improvisation that may be vital for a resolution at that moment.

CENTRALISING POWER

There is a tendency in crises, when we do not see progress from others, to feel the need to assume control. We believe that we can do better and that by transferring power to ourselves we can single-handedly deal with the situation more effectively than we could as a group.

Unfortunately, this form of centralisation (and the accompanying power games) is often a side-effect of a crisis in projects.

THINKING AND ACTING IN THE PAST

It is likely that a crisis, in its totality, is of a type that you have not directly experienced before. However, human nature means that it is also likely that you will rely on recovery mechanisms you have deployed in the past. Tackling a novel crisis that requires quick and decisive action through drawing on past solutions is not only likely to be ineffective but might exacerbate the crisis. We are habitual creatures, and we tend to rely on our past experiences and schemas of action. However, these past-informed habits may not fit the present crisis. Being aware of this may enable us to focus more clearly on new, more creative solutions to the current crisis.

HINDSIGHT BIAS

People tend to revise the probabilities of an event or phenomenon happening after it has happened. They exaggerate the extent to which that event or phenomenon might have been predicted beforehand. This tendency is known as hindsight bias (sometimes colloquially called the 'I-knew-it-all-along effect') and is one of the most widely studied decision traps due to its ubiquitous nature.

This cognitive bias is remarkably robust across all populations and in all situations. For example, it has been found in people's views on general knowledge questions, in predictions of sporting events and political elections, in business and organisational decision-making and in medical diagnoses (Christensen-Szalanski and Willham 1991).

The effect of hindsight bias is that people believe they knew the outcome of an event after that event has already happened. There are some factors at play in hindsight bias (Pohl and Erdfelder 2004). First, people tend to misremember or distort their previous predictions. Second, people regard events as having been inevitable all along and, finally, people assume events could have been foreseen. Where all three factors are in play at the same time, hindsight bias is very likely to occur.

In organisational activities, hindsight bias can distort decision-making profoundly. For example, it significantly distorts the evaluations of strategic decisions in organisations and, as a result, distorts projections for the future (Bukszar and Connolly 1988). Elsewhere, with start-ups, entrepreneurs who recalled their experiences with previous experiences were over-confident in their belief that they would be successful in the future as a result of hindsight bias (Cassar and Craig 2009).

TUNNEL VISION

Under increased stress, the scope of our radar narrows and shortens. Our minds tend to focus on single actions, and the insufficiency of response in alleviating the situation is compensated by a further fixation on executing it, sometimes over and over. Such fixation may prevent us from remaining sensitive to the bigger picture of what is going on around us.

KEY ENABLERS TO RECOVERING

The behaviours that typically emerge in crises are ones that need to be actively managed, in a mindful manner. Usually, the goals, when faced with a crisis, are its immediate resolution and 'damage control'. This is important, but so too is a necessary shift in the way the crisis is managed. As quickly as possible, the recovery stage needs to be initiated.

PROJECT CONTINUITY

This book is very much about the 'soft' aspects of project management, about behaviours and applied practice. Nevertheless, one cannot ignore the need for some mindless structure that can be relied upon quickly. Every crisis response involves business continuity planning. For project work, this continuity plan defines which functions in the project are critical to address, protect, and maintain. For example, in a software development project, a vital function might be the 'testing environment' in which sections of code are brought together and functionally evaluated. If these critical functions come to a standstill, the whole project could be put on hold. In a crisis, such functions deserve special attention. So, a plan can be activated quickly, even if that means in a mindless checklist manner.

CHECKLISTS

In a crisis, the resulting stress and 'tunnel vision' may be countered by the relative 'automation' of a checklist. A checklist should not replace human situated cognition, but it can help to probe the situation and aid a project manager's state of mindfulness. A useful checklist is one that is:

- Short and simple. Simplicity forces project managers to accept a stimulus and to interpret.
- Focussed. It aims at critical functions of a project. Insignificant components of a project are not checklisted.
- Practical. It only offers probes based on actions that are doable and feasible.

CLOSENESS

We might have all the necessary plans in place, but because of the unfamiliar character of a crisis, we are not ready to exercise those plans, let alone be reflective and creative. The question this raises is how to sensitise a project team for a crisis, in a safe environment, before the crisis happens. One answer lies in simulating worst-case scenarios. Crisis simulations have the great benefit of getting close to extreme situations. Playing through worst-case settings, to test one's endurance and adaptability in a 'live' but safe environment is at the core of simulating crises.

It is a puzzle that, in many projects where substantial value is at stake, planning and preparation involve tools and techniques that do not incorporate the emotive side of managing uncertainty. Most planning approaches advocated in project management seem to exclude the behavioural side of a crisis. If you can, simulate a crisis that allows you to receive immediate feedback on crucial stakeholders' behaviours and skills under high-stress conditions. It is too late to test out aspects of mindful behaviour when a real crisis is already unfolding.

TIGER TEAMS

When a crisis strikes, seeking an outsider's perspective can be vital. Internal politics tend to take over in the middle of a major problem as people can become insensitive and defensive and may entrench themselves in their silos. If we wish to find a swift solution to avert disaster, this silo mentality needs to be broken up. Tiger Teams (whether they are called that or go by some other name) can deliberately be set up as high-performing teams aiming to reconcile potentially opposing views and facilitating solution-finding in out-of-control situations.

They need to be on stand-by or to hover around a project, monitoring the situation and ready to provide the project manager with support. They can be parachuted in when the situation warrants it. A Tiger Team must not replace the project manager but support the project manager in the following:

- Listening and asking questions from multiple perspectives about what is happening and yet not rushing to conclusions despite the pressure to act quickly.
- Imagining worst-case implications, together with the details of complex, potentially dynamically changing, tasks.

- Suppressing members' egos in terms of 'knowing the answer' yet remaining inquisitive in creating options.
- Willingness to break existing rules and processes, with the ability to think outside of the usual methods of operation.
- Skills to create solutions that work at the technical, process and human levels.
- Ability to maintain a continuously high level of focus and intensity of action.
- Maintaining all this to achieve rapid project recovery while operating within challenging timeframes under the 'spotlight' of senior management.

In projects, the role of the project manager is frequently an 'everything' function. They are often expected to switch seamlessly from managing 'business as usual' to being a crisis manager. The shift from normality to a crisis-like situation, however, can be difficult for us who are emotionally and structurally attached to the project. Instead, a set of seasoned managers, possibly currently involved in other projects but with scope to provide the necessary support to a project in trouble, can be used to ensure that valuable input.

MINDFUL PRACTICES

TIGER TEAMS

In Intel development projects, unexpected problems occasionally require some form of trouble-shooting. At the centre of initiating a problem-solving process are so-called 'Tiger Teams' – ad hoc small groups of subject matter experts coming together to deal with routine, every day, problem-solving (and also crises). These Tiger Teams are often 'self-selected', with experts from within and outside the domain in which the project resides. Availability is driven by an interest to engage with a challenging problem. The length of engagement is initially estimated, but there is flexibility in extending the time the experts belong to the team until the problem is solved:

> *A Tiger Team would be something where you bring together a set of people for a short period to fix an issue. For example, it could be a system that's in production already, but it's gone wrong, or where you've got multiple users and the order has gone down. Or it could be an area within the project that needs special attention, and you want to bring in people may be outside of the project team where you need additional skill sets to help get over the critical challenge that's facing you right now ...*

Setting up a Tiger Team for a limited time requires flexibility in the organisation to provide expertise on an ad hoc basis. This is because critical problems are generally not planned for, they emerge. Cost-centred thinking about lending resources to deal with a temporary problem is not a constraint at Intel.

Another factor to consider is uncertainty in how long a Tiger Team is likely to be deployed. Without having certainty about when the problem will be solved, stakeholders and cost centres need to be informed, and they also need to show time flexibility, allowing their scarce resources to be engaged with the problem until they are no longer required:

> *you'd set out a goal to start with to come back in a week and have a status review. Generally, in a Tiger Team, you might be sending emails every day about what's happening, so people are aware of the progress you're making: to your stakeholders if there's a business impact; and to the resource managers, so they understand the progress. After a while, you'll get to a point where you've resolved it, or you understand the issue, and then the recommendation comes out of that.*

What is mindful about it? A Tiger Team, often referred to as a response team or a 'hit squad', provide additional mindful capabilities in times of extreme complexity and uncertainty: a crisis.

Tiger Teams are not just a collection of experts; they are experts driven by a purpose or problem statement. Their strengths are to initiate an open and honest constructive 'struggle' to understand multidisciplinary, cross-functional problems by reconciling different perspectives and allowing holistic big picture thinking. A well-functioning Tiger Team exhibits the following characteristics:

- Openness, trust and respect: everyone is encouraged to speak freely from his or her disciplinary perspective. An opinion is neither right nor wrong; all opinions are respected.
- Common goal: the goal is to get the problem resolved, and the common goal of trouble-shooting a multi-disciplinary problem is prioritised.
- Commitment: although Tiger Teams are a temporary form of troubleshooting, every expert shows a desire to contribute to problem-solving.

LOGISTICAL INDEPENDENCE

The resources that have been provided for project 'normality' may not be the most suitable to help in a crisis. Indeed, one may argue that the resources deployed in the incubation phase of a crisis have been insufficient to prevent it from occurring in the first place. The Tiger Team has to draw on a pool of readily or quickly made available resources, be it people or additional funds. This access to resources should be detached from the daily business of the project. Lengthy, otherwise sensible, change-related processes need to be unhooked or circumvented.

Nevertheless, this does not imply that the provision and deployment of resources to stem a crisis should be allowed to unfold haphazardly. Similarly, the question of how this extra resource is paid for should not add to the difficulties of the project. Preparations should ideally be made in advance of any crisis occurring. Arrangements may, for example, include the provision of a budget for these resources (as yet unspecified, since the nature of any future crisis is unknown) in advance of their mobilisation. As we encounter time-consuming 'blame-games' in crises, the risk of a silo- mentality associated with lengthy and often futile searches for root causes could be overcome by switching to a contractual model that 'shares' the costs of managing a crisis, regardless of which party 'caused' it. This focuses minds on solutions, not blame.

LEADING THE ART OF RECOVERING

A crisis in a project is often perceived as threatening, a period of confusion which requires an urgent remedy. It is at these moments that project managers need to be 'leaders' as their staff will look to them to 'do something'. The challenge for leaders in projects is to 'bring things back to normal'.

Readiness to initiate a radical shift in the mode of management is required in advance; from a phase characterised by shock, confrontation and increased response rigidity, to one of reflection, collaboration and adaptation. Leadership is necessary to prepare stakeholders for such an essential transition and to facilitate a move from potential inaction and rigidity towards recovery.

READYING STAKEHOLDERS

Stakeholders need to be educated for 'when' it happens, not 'if'. Of course, if at all possible, we want to prevent a crisis from ever happening, and this is the focus of all the planning that goes into projects. The result of this effort is an unspoken assumption that failure will not or can not happen, and this makes readying stakeholders for engaging with a crisis all the more difficult. Doing so is an implicit acknowledgement of failure. It also costs time and effort to prepare stakeholders for a crisis in the absence of one. Why prepare for something that has not happened yet and may not happen anyway? We have to allow time and effort, often in advance of the execution of the project, for techniques that would enable key stakeholders (for example, the client) to rehearse a crisis, and to test the response capability to deal with one. Whether such rehearsing involves the development of plans, simulations of scenarios, or storytelling does not matter, as long as the approach helps to sensitise people to the emotive factors of a crisis. Words in isolation, in the form of a plan – dry, impersonal – are inadequate to convey the behavioural side of a crisis.

JUST-WORLD HYPOTHESIS

The just-world hypothesis (also called the just-world phenomenon, bias, belief, or fallacy) is a cognitive bias where people view the social environment as, primarily, a fair environment (Lerner 1980). The result of this is that people will devalue the experience of victims within a social environment. This is because people want to believe the world is essentially a fair place so rationalise or explain-away injustices, often blaming people who are victims for their own misfortune. This is the case even when those victims have little or no control over events. People take unjustifiable credit when things go well, believing this to be entirely or mainly as a result of their hard-work, superior intelligence or some other personal capacity.

It has been suggested that the just world fallacy is held by people for several reasons (Hafer and Bègue 2005). Chief among these appears to be that people fear facing vulnerability. Because people fear to be victims themselves, when they hear of other people becoming victims of some event, they try to assign blame for the event on the victim's behaviour. A classic example of this is victim-blaming rape victims. This allows people to believe they can avoid becoming victims by avoiding certain behaviours associated with victims. Another explanation for the just-world phenomenon is that people are seeking to reduce the anxiety they feel caused by the world's injustices. Believing people are responsible for their misfortunes allows people to believe the world is fair and just.

Within organisations, the just world fallacy can arise in a variety of contexts. It can impact on business ethics where lower ethical standards are found among managers who have a strong belief in the just world hypothesis (Ashkanasy et al. 2006). It can also be found in recruitment and promotion and, through this, power differentials in organisational hierarchies (Pfeffer 2010). This effect can also be felt more widely across organisations. For example, when competitors go out of business, managers in an organisation may feel confident that they can take over that competitor's business or, in some other way, capitalise on that competitor's demise failing to see that the reasons for the competitor's failure may also affect their organisation too. The just-world fallacy means that managers know the failure of competitors to be as a result of their own failing rather than something systemic (Pfeffer 2010).

BEING RELUCTANT TO PRESS THE PANIC BUTTON

We need to set expectations in circumstances where people look to them for guidance. The temptation is to convey messages that the situation is likely to turn out for the best. On the one hand, this optimistic perspective instils confidence and motivates, but it might also lead to illusions of control and thus to blind spots. If people absorb the belief that everything will go well, they may become less vigilant and less adaptive in their understanding. The result may be greater rigidity and inaction in response to the unfolding situation.

On the other hand, portraying a doomsday scenario encourages fatalistic behaviour, in which people sit back and let fate play its cards. It is down to the leader to find an appropriate balance in setting expectations between being too optimistic and pessimistic. Generally, we tend to underestimate the severity of a crisis and overestimate our capabilities to deal with one, so we should tend to look at challenging over-optimism.

RESTRAINT BIAS

Restraint bias is a well-recognised cognitive bias that describes the tendency of people to overestimate their ability to control their basic impulses, temptations and desires (Nordgren et al. 2009). This leads people to increase their exposure to these temptations and urges and, in so doing, increasing the likelihood that they will succumb to them. This arises due to a particular type of empathy gap effect in that people are unable to empathise with their future mind-state and thus fail to consider how their mental processes will operate at a future date.

Restraint bias manifests itself in many ways in everyday life. Some examples include the inability to avoid smoking and the tendency of people to become over fatigued (Nordgren et al. 2009).

In marketing, consumer restraint bias is used to positive effect for businesses seeking to promote their products and services. Indeed, in some cases, advertising relies on restraint bias to encourage consumers to place themselves in the way of temptation and, hence, to consume (Campbell and Warren 2015).

BEING HESITANT TO CENTRALISE

Defensive retreats often go hand-in-hand with the urge to centralise. We may lose trust in other people because they did not prevent the crisis from happening in the first place. As a result, we may be tempted to rein in many tasks they have previously delegated. Be warned! If we do this, we may find it challenging to focus on what a leader is supposed to do in a crisis – facilitate an understanding of the problem and its solution. Being bogged down in detail prevents us from maintaining sensitivity to what is happening.

A crisis requires courageous action, yet it is not up to us to take all the brave steps. Indeed, we need to let go and facilitate action where it matters, close to the problem, and develop the commitment to respond in the most sensible and valuable way. Such determination cannot be taken for granted, given that people may retreat into their shells and may exhibit rigidity, only responding to cover themselves. Such self-preservation in times of upheaval is common (and understandable) and needs to be addressed by project leaders. This commitment should be supported by the provision of an extensive response repository for those 'firefighters'. Vast power needs to be channelled down to front-line staff, while leaders remain sensitive to what is going on and intervene only when necessary. However, interventions may be interpreted as a sign of distrust or suggest that power is centralised and does not require any response from those closest to the problem. If we intervene, we need to explain and clarify the purpose of such intervention.

MAINTAINING TRUST

A crisis can be deliberately triggered because of hidden agendas. Crises encourage us to be more defensive, and walls are consequently built around silos (defensive retreats). In this situation, trust can evaporate. Trust can be established (or re-established) by us if we focus on showing compassion and concern. In a crisis, people may think that their work and importance is diminished. If, for example, a Tiger Team has been parachuted in to mediate, other stakeholders may find themselves side-lined. Show 'real' concern to every project team member. Consider the necessity of shifting power, for example, to Tiger Teams and address and explain the rationale for the decisions and leadership interventions that have been made.

Showing concern goes hand-in-hand with being honest and transparent. Communicate that there are conflicting perspectives and expectations; be honest about the pressure that people are under but show optimism that solutions are feasible. Provide pertinent information in 'real-time'. Outdated information may be misinterpreted as following a hidden agenda.

However, although communication in a crisis is essential, it needs to be controlled. Unreliable information may only add to rumours and fuel false impressions. We want to air their opinions, especially when their own positions and departments are involved. Unwarranted speculations about what is happening or what might be done are detrimental if project managers fail to control them. We should offer our project members valid information and plenty of opportunities to voice their opinions, but information (or a lack thereof) should not be turned into ammunition to serve political agendas. Facilitate communication in an open manner by assuring the reliability of its content.

MANAGE BEHAVIOUR, NOT PLANS

Crisis management plans or checklists – outlining sets of predefined, 'mechanistically' and thus mindlessly performed actions – are there for a reason, to provide some form of structure and order in an environment perceived as being chaotic. However, these plans can be a double-edged sword. On the positive side, they help to trigger behaviours quickly and efficiently. Conversely, they may suppress situated human cognition. If plans do not adequately match the situation at hand, we may blindly walk into disaster. We constantly need to reflect on the appropriateness of plans and check-lists and their execution. If a plan does not appear to match the situation as we perceive it, we must deviate from it. Ultimately, we manage behaviour and plans are there to support this, not vice versa.

CHANNEL RESOURCES TO WHERE THEY ARE NEEDED FIRST

Contingency plans do help to pinpoint critical functions in a project. The question of 'What must not go further wrong?' – a question often not asked – drives a greater understanding of the most vital resource allocation. In a crisis, we may throw resources at anything that poses a threat. A much more effective course of action is to prioritise the deployment of resources to where they matter. For example, if we talk about a project that delivers a range of benefits (e.g. functions), then systematically categorising what must or should not go wrong (any further) is a sensible approach. The 'must not' requires the most considerable attention and forces clear prioritisation.

LEARNING FROM CRISES

A crisis in which a project stands at the edge of disaster requires reflection and learning. However, we often want to detach ourselves from this uncomfortable experience. The urge to forget and move on to other tasks can leave the potential for learning untapped. Learning from a crisis, if it happens, often takes the form of analysing, documenting and allocating root causes, with the purpose of standardising responses to any future crisis. In its own way, this appears to be a sensible solution unless we operate in an environment in which crises unfold in random patterns. However, expecting a similar predicament to hit you another time may, in itself, form a root cause for future failure.

Learning should go beyond the past, and learners – us – should be reluctant to replace valuable human cognition with yet another additional layer of prescribed process and procedure without a strong rationale for doing so. But how? Storytelling is considered a potent mechanism to convey rich context – an event or crisis – and provide a platform for the 'listeners' to develop their learning.

A 'good' story:

- is authentic and one that the listener is familiar with and can relate to;
- combines words with images and audio to appeal to all our senses;
- is connected to an organisational narrative or a bridge is built so that the story is linked to the context of the listener;
- provides a clear structure, often helped by a timeline;
- is simple and relatively short, to maintain attention.

People naturally make sense of experience through storytelling, and therefore, it can be a very powerful learning tool. Storytelling done well can encourage reflection, inspire current and future collaborative approaches, stimulate enquiry and help to build knowledge and understanding. Additionally, cultural and emotional contexts can be understood and acknowledged as being important. It is only one way to reflect upon practice and find ways of making sense of crises but, compared with dry, codified knowledge that may never be read, it is a very accessible means of learning. Indeed, it happens anyway. In social gatherings, we may trade 'war stories' of what went wrong in projects we have been involved in.

LAW OF TRIVIALITY

Initially observed by the British naval historian, Cyril Northcote Parkinson, the law of triviality describes the tendency for people to devote inordinate amounts of time and effort to thinking about and resolving minor, trivial details while ignoring significant or crucial matters (Keller and Meaney 2017). This differs from the more famous Parkinson's law, where Parkinson observed that work expands to use up the amount of time allocated for it. The law of triviality has become known as 'bikeshedding' because Parkinson invented a fictional committee to approve the plans for a nuclear power station, but they spent inordinate amounts of time focused on the trivial task of thinking about the material used in the construction of the bikesheds.

In organisations, the law of triviality can manifest itself in many ways. The most obvious one is that organisations tend to give disproportionate weight to trivial issues. This can lead to the time being devoted to any particular item being inversely proportional to the amount of money involved and the amount of energy, effort and time generated by changes being inversely proportional to the complexity of those changes.

There would seem to be some underlying reasons explaining behaviours consistent with the law of triviality. Perhaps the most important of these is that people prefer to focus on and form an opinion about problems that are easier to understand than more complex issues. Connected with this, making decisions about more essential matters brings with it more responsibility for those decisions, and people often seek to avoid or dodge responsibility for decisions. Often, managers will assume that people responsible for complex decisions will already have done their job and assessed the issue. Finally, people are drawn to trivial issues as these require less time, effort and money to resolve.

MINDFUL PRACTICES

CHALLENGING WAYS OF WORKING

In The Technology Partnership (TTP), it is the responsibility of project managers to explore beyond the 'known expertise'. They do this through extensive empowerment but this only works if access to additional know-how is provided:

If you need particular expertise on a project, you can pull it from anywhere in the company.

The provision of additional expertise gives project managers multiple perspectives but does not constitute a delegation of responsibility. Deference to expertise, as exercised at TTP, is aimed at:

- seeing your project from a different perspective;
- encouraging scepticism;
- acknowledging adversarial views;
- challenging your assumptions.

All of this is done in the interest of making fewer assumptions, noticing more and ignoring less. This is all about addressing risk blindness – the ability to notice blind spots – and is carried out at TTP using an elaborate process of 'peer reviews'. This process acts as a 'sensor' to highlight blind spots and, in TTP, is carried out by independent functions:

When we do a technical review, we usually invite someone who is not involved directly on the project because they can come and often spot things that someone too close to it cannot see.

TTP's peer-reviews are not designed to 'check' whether project managers are compliant with the organisation's rules and procedures. Instead, they are designed to make project managers think about what they are doing and, most importantly, why:

It is to stand back and think about what you are doing.
They will ask you difficult questions and spot things that you might not have thought of yourself.
You start to recognise some early signs [of failure].

Even in times of urgency, where there might be a temptation to rely on an 'autopilot' mentality and replicate what one has been doing in the past, deference to expertise provides a 'sanity-check':

It's taking a step back to try and see whether you are doing the right thing.

What is mindful about it? The implementation of such a peer-review system has its challenges, too. Project managers might see it as 'Big Brother' watching over them and telling them what is right and what is wrong. Or, they might rely on their peers as a crutch to help them make decisions rather than making decisions for themselves. This is why challenging assumptions to detect risk blindness, should not include the imposition of 'answers'. In TTP, the peer-reviewing mechanism acknowledges the 'folly of imposed solutions' and offers support to make a project manager think and be creative in his or her problem-solving – it is *not* about making the project manager obey. This is in stark contrast with many other organisations, where 'auditing' is used to ensure that employees remain within a supposedly self-evidently correct management framework. Not so TTP, which uses expertise 'just' to inform.

THE IMPACT OF RECOVERING ON RELATIONSHIPS

A crisis is a time of high emotion with the project viability at stake. The threat of stopping or suspending the work and the resulting potential damage to the reputation of all the parties involved hangs like a dark cloud over the heads of stakeholders. It is vital that crisis management efforts are not only targeted at the most vulnerable and most critical functions but also at those people who are most affected (these are not necessarily those in the thick of it). Relationships are at stake.

ESTABLISH CLARITY

The antithesis of a defensive retreat is to break down barriers and share information freely while being sure to control the accuracy of the information. Sharing information should be done with the help of clear contact points. Stakeholders should not need to seek out sources of information on crisis updates or how the crisis is being dealt with. An obvious choice is the project manager, who is most often closest to the evolving situation and has the most unobstructed view of events.

LISTENING

An important aspect of crisis management is that of caring through listening. Listening is not as easy as it may seem, though. Reflective listening involves both content checking and feeling checking. Content checking implies mutual acknowledgement of each other's understanding of what has been said. Restating content provides reassurance of a shared understanding. Feeling and checking is not so much about the content but the emotions, involving feedback and reflection on each other's emotional state.

As with so many skills that are important in a crisis, listening, to show that one cares for another's content and emotions is not without barriers:

- Anticipating a message: you may already think or expect in advance what the person is going to say and hence you might interrupt them.
- Rehearsing an answer: while the person is trying to convey their message, you may already be thinking about an answer, and thus you will not give them the attention they deserve.
- Thought wandering: a cue by a person may make your thoughts wander off. This may lead to misinterpretation and the need for that person to repeat the message.
- Premature conclusion: you may already have come up with a conclusion, although the message is incomplete.

COLLECTIVELY OWNING A CRISIS

A crisis, regardless of whether sudden or creeping, is often caused by a multitude of factors. Hence, searching for a single root cause is often a futile exercise; not having a root cause in place does not negate the collective 'ownership' of the crisis, though. However, ownership is not to be mistaken for accountability. A project manager may be held accountable for what he or she does to resolve the crisis by providing timely feedback and measuring progress toward recovery. Ownership, though, is the obligation of the collected stakeholders. Ownership is created by establishing collaboration and a sense of partnership in the belief that recovering from a crisis is in the best interest of all parties. Commitment from all parties involved to engage in timely (and often costly) actions of troubleshooting is highly valuable and provides a sense of cohesion.

THINK LONG-TERM RELATIONSHIP

A characteristic of a defensive retreat is myopia: short term thinking. We tend to ask ourselves during a crisis how to recover from it in the short-term. Our horizon may not move beyond the phase of recovery. However, not only is the project at risk but also the long-term relationships with stakeholders. Questions need to be asked about what happens after a successful recovery, and how (potentially) damaged trust between stakeholders can be re-established. It is dangerous to wait until after the crisis has passed to consider how groups and individuals could and should work together in the longer term. Projects are (by definition) transient and, although it is difficult when current work is in turmoil, it is important to consider future projects and the sustainable working relationships that will be necessary to support them.

HYPERBOLIC DISCOUNTING

A behaviour commonly found among people is that their perceptions of rewards vary over time. It is found that the way people value a relative reward or return at some point in the future differs when it is compared to a valuation of that reward at an earlier date. This non-consistent, time-based valuation is described by the theory of hyperbolic discounting (Frederick and Loewenstein 2002). It is called hyperbolic discounting because the behaviour observed is found to invariably follow a hyperbolic curve (Bradshaw et al. 1976). This is because rewards in the here and now are weighted by people more heavily than future ones. If the reward is far into the future, then its value diminishes to virtually nothing. This kind of delay discounting helps to explain impulsive behaviour by people. The tendency to seek immediate gratification can be seen in all sorts of situations, such as craving a cigarette, over-indulging in food or alcohol, and general procrastination.

Primarily, hyperbolic discounting exists because of the nature of time – people have limited time available to them and are geared to instinctively recognise that resources stored for the future cannot be used if they are unable to avail themselves of it. This is because the future is uncertain, and the distant future is highly unpredictable and results in a present bias – consume now (Azfar 1999).

SHARING THE BURDEN OF RECOVERY

It is tempting in a crisis to look for a root cause and allocate the burden – costs, emotions, responsibility for recovering from it – to those believed to be the triggering factor for the predicament. This search for single-point failures and single-point accountability is often already manifested in the choice of contract. Projects most often rely on a 'traditional' type of contract, with a focus on the position of one party to the contract concerning the actions of the other parties. Essentially, this can set up an adversarial relationship, with each party to the contract protecting its position and looking to maximise its benefit. The agreement itself can encourage and exacerbate the adversarial stance taken by the various parties delivering the project. The focus can shift to personal gain rather than the goals of the project. This is the antithesis of project partnering wherein there is an implicit (and often explicit) assumption that all parties involved in the project are committed to a single goal while recognising the different and shared needs of the various organisations involved. This is well-understood in many project environments and has led to the development of a variety of alternative, more collaborative, contract forms. With collaboration comes the incentive to share the costs of tackling problems. Typical of these types of contracts is some form of pain/gain share agreement, whereby the costs of failing to meet milestones or objectives are shared among project participants. By the same token, the project is delivered below budget, or early, then all participants can share this better than expected outcome.

The key of a partnering contract is to encourage swift and efficient collaborative problem-solving while avoiding the sometimes crippling transaction costs that are so often the outcome of more traditional contract forms. These transaction costs have two effects on the project: they can mire the project participants in bickering over where the fault lies, rather than focusing on resolution, and they involve inordinate record-keeping and costly arguments over who is to blame, often resulting in protracted legal disputes long after the work has been completed.

To avoid some of these problems, collaborative, partnering-type projects will typically be 'open-book' whereby the client and the project team can view each other's project documents. There are two main justifications for this: project parties have to trust each other, and it avoids the need for costly claims. Hidden agendas are removed, and the project staff and workers start to focus on the needs of the project rather than those of their organisations.

CELEBRATE A VICTORY

Overcoming a crisis is a feat to celebrate. Crises do occur and often are not preventable. They are high-pressure situations in which emotions take the upper hand and recovering from one deserves recognition. However, it is tempting to lay the memories of such a painful phase of the life cycle to rest, to forget and to move on. Stakeholders need to recognise their successful recovery and rebuild potentially damaged relationships. By celebrating victory over a crisis, negative connotations about its occurrence can, at least to some extent, be alleviated.

NEGATIVITY BIAS

Negativity bias (sometimes known as the negativity effect) describes the tendency of people to give more weight to negatively perceived events than they do to positively viewed events, even where those positive events are as equally important (or even better) than the negative. In other words, 'bad … is stronger than good' to a scale of as much as three times (Baumeister et al. 2001). Adverse events can take many forms, from everyday activities to significant life traumas. Whatever they are, they will almost always outweigh similar good events in terms of their importance to people. Events may be outcomes of close relationships, social networks or physical events.

There are several explanations for people's innate negativity bias. It may be that we pay more attention to adverse events rather than positive ones. Another explanation is that we learn more from adverse events than positive. From an organisational point of view, people also tend to make decisions based on harmful data rather than positive data and people are more motivated to complete tasks if they think they will lose something rather than if they believe they will gain something.

In organisations, negativity bias manifests itself in a host of ways. In particular, it has been found to affect people in their interest in doing something new or seeking to innovate. This is because managers and other organisational decision-makers tend to recall when innovation and change failed more readily than when it succeeded (Luthans et al. 2011). In addition, workplace discipline and subsequent productivity can be impacted by negativity bias (Skaggs et al. 2018).

APPLE – A SUCCESS OF RECOVERING

In 1997, Apple was about 90 days from going bankrupt. The Silicon Valley pioneer was founded in 1976, with a mission to mass-market small, simple and, most of all, affordable computers. In the mid-1980s, Apple failed to compete with Microsoft. Lack of new ideas, and failed products, as well as the gamble of takeovers of ailing companies such as Next took its toll. The company was burning through money and capital. By 1997, Apple had lost $867 million, and its value reduced to $3 billion.

In July 1997, Steve Jobs returned to Apple (after he had been ousted in 1985). His first step to get Apple out of the red was criticised by many: he aligned Apple with his key competitor Microsoft. Bill Gates, the CEO of Microsoft, and Jobs announced cooperation that would allow the release of an updated Mac version of Microsoft Office, as well as a significant investment programme in Apple of around £150 million. Jobs argued:

> If we want to move forward and see Apple healthy and prospering again, we have to let go of a few things here. We have to let go of this notion that for Apple to win, Microsoft has to lose.

(Shontell 2010)

On such solid footing, feeding off the successful products of Microsoft, Jobs imposed his authority, confidence and good ideas to lead Apple into profitability. The iMac G3 was introduced in 1998, and defined the hallmark of Apple ever since, pioneering in technology, underlined by simplicity and appeal in design. The 'all-in-one' iMac became a hit with 800,000 units sold in the first five months. The iMac was followed by the iPod in 2003 and the debut of the iPhone in 2007. At the launch of the iPhone, Apple was worth $73.4 billion.

In many 'failing' project-based organisations, the first reaction may well be to 'entrench' a company's capabilities and culture to deliver projects, to think and act more mindlessly by reinvigorating the past that may well have triggered a crisis in the first place. Like Apple, an organisation needs to break with the past, free itself of past crises, be reluctant to press the panic button, and decisively shape a future that creates opportunities. The discomfort in mindfully shaping a prospect is to empower employees to look past a crisis and engage stakeholders in the process of creating mindful behaviours; creating sustained commitment towards and embracing uncertainty beyond what is known from the past.

TOWARDS AN ART OF RECOVERING

A crisis is something to be anticipated. Uncertainty will sometimes slip through our defences, and complexity will do the rest in creating a state that threatens the viability of a project. This threat increases the pressure for us to act mindlessly, to jump to conclusions, and emotions will run high. Counterproductive behaviour is to be expected and needs to be managed carefully. Defensive retreats need to be broken down and objectivity re-established. Additional capabilities, for example, the use of a Tiger Team, may need to be parachuted in, to provide mindful interventions.

The previous sections provided a range of suggestions on how to cope with a crisis in a project. These suggestions – and to remind the reader, these are just suggestions – are encapsulated in the following statements:

Reflection *How well do the following statements characterise your project? For each item, select one box only that best reflects your conclusion.*

	Fully agree	Neither agree nor disagree			Fully disagree
We have a common understanding that crises are a normal, yet infrequent, part of project life.	1	2	3	4	5
A crisis includes the management of behaviours, and less so of plans.	1	2	3	4	5
We prepare for crises by experiencing them via simulations and do not rely exclusively on a written crisis management plan.	1	2	3	4	5

	Fully agree	Neither agree nor disagree			Fully disagree
We use independent personnel to give objectivity and help develop solutions in crises.	1	2	3	4	5
We accept that decision rigidity may hamper the development of an effective response, and we provide appropriate levels of freedom to enable creative solutions to emerge.	1	2	3	4	5
We try to care for every stakeholder by keeping them informed of the evolving situation and addressing their particular needs.	1	2	3	4	5

	Fully agree	Neither agree nor disagree			Fully disagree
Managing the full flow of information is critically important in a crisis. We provide relevant and timely information in a calm, orderly, and controlled manner.	1	2	3	4	5
We recognise the importance of sharing the burden of a crisis.	1	2	3	4	5
We reflect on our behaviour in a crisis to learn to deal with future events.	1	2	3	4	5

Scoring: Add the numbers. If you score higher than 27, your mindful capability to recover from a crisis is good. If you score 27 or lower, please consider how you may be able to enhance your capability to manage a crisis.

REFERENCES

Ashkanasy, N. M., C. A. Windsor, and L. K. Treviño. 2006. "Bad Apples in Bad Barrels Revisited: Cognitive Moral Development, Just World Beliefs, Rewards, and Ethical Decision-Making." *Business Ethics Quarterly* 16(4): 449–73.

Azfar, O. 1999. "Rationalizing Hyperbolic Discounting." *Journal of Economic Behavior and Organization* 38(2): 245–52.

Babad, E., and Y. Katz. 1991. "Wishful Thinking—Against All Odds." *Journal of Applied Social Psychology* 21(23): 1921–38.

Baumeister, R. F., E. Bratslavsky, C. Finkenauer, and K. D. Vohs. 2001. "Bad Is Stronger Than Good." *Review of General Psychology* 5(4): 323–70.

Bradshaw, C. M., E. Szabadi, and P. Bevan. 1976. "Behavior of Humans in Variable-Interval Schedules of Reinforcement." *Journal of the Experimental Analysis of Behavior* 26(2): 135–41.

Bukszar, E., and T. Connolly. 1988. "Hindsight Bias and Strategic Choice: Some Problems in Learning from Experience." *Academy of Management Journal* 31(3): 628–41.

Campbell, M. C., and C. Warren. 2015. "The Progress Bias in Goal Pursuit: When One Step Forward Seems Larger than One Step Back." *Journal of Consumer Research* 41(5): 1316–31.

Cassar, G., and J. Craig. 2009. "An Investigation of Hindsight Bias in Nascent Venture Activity." *Journal of Business Venturing* 24(2): 149–64.

Christensen-Szalanski, J. J. J., and C. F. Willham. 1991. "The Hindsight Bias: A Meta-Analysis." *Organizational Behavior and Human Decision Processes* 48(1): 147–68.

Frederick, S., and G. Loewenstein. 2002. "Time Discounting and Time Preference: A Critical Review." *Journal of Economic Literature* 40: 351–401.

Galai, D., and O. Sade. 2006. "The 'Ostrich Effect' and the Relationship between the Liquidity and the Yields of Financial Assets." *Journal of Business* 79(5): 2741–59.

Hafer, C. L., and L. Bègue. 2005. "Experimental Research on Just-World Theory: Problems, Developments, and Future Challenges." *Psychological Bulletin* 131(1): 128–67.

Karlsson, N., G. Loewenstein, and D. Seppi. 2009. "The Ostrich Effect: Selective Attention to Information." *Journal of Risk and Uncertainty* 38(2): 95–115.

Keller, S., and M. Meaney. 2017. "High-Performing Teams: A Timeless Leadership Topic." *McKinsey Quarterly* 1(3): 81–87.

Kutsch, E., and M. Hall. 2005. "Intervening Conditions on the Management of Project Risk: Dealing with Uncertainty in Information Technology Projects." *International Journal of Project Management* 23: 8.

Lerner, M. J. 1980. *The Belief in A Just World: A Fundamental Delusion.* New York: Plenum.

Luthans, F., C. M. Youssef, and S. L. Rawski. 2011. "A Tale of Two Paradigms: The Impact of Psychological Capital and Reinforcing Feedback on Problem Solving and Innovation." *Journal of Organizational Behavior Management* 31(4): 333–50.

Nordgren, L. F., F. Van Harreveld, and J. Van Der Pligt.. 2009. "The Restraint Bias: How the Illusion of Self-Restraint Promotes Impulsive Behavior." *Psychological Science* 20(12): 1523–28.

Pfeffer, J. 2010. *Power: Why Some People Have It and Others Don't.* New York: Harper Business.

Pohl, R. F., and E. Erdfelder. 2004. "Hindsight Bias." In: *Cognitive Illusions: A Handbook on Fallacies and Biases in Thinking, Judgement and Memory*, edited by Rüdiger F. Pohl, 363–78. Hove: Psychology Press.

Shontell, A. 2010. "TIP OF THE DAY: 'We Have To Let Go Of This Notion That For Apple To Win, Microsoft Has To Lose." Business Insider. 2010. https://www.businessinsider.com/tip-of-the-day-we-have-to-let-go-of-this-notion-that-for-apple-to-win-microsoft-has-to-lose-2010-9?r=US&IR=T.

Skaggs, B. C., C. C. Manz, M. C. B. Lyle, and C. L. Pearce. 2018. "On the Folly of Punishing A while Hoping for A: Exploring Punishment in Organizations." *Journal of Organizational Behavior* 39(6): 812–15.

CHAPTER EIGHT

Roads to resilience

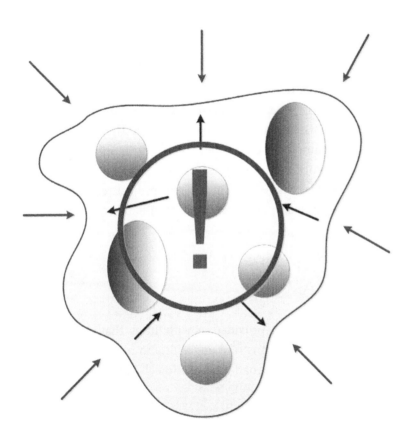

CONTENTS

A s we have seen, projects are constantly challenged by the effects
of uncertainty. Based on experience and having a memory of
past events, projects build up defences that are continually maintained
and updated in an attempt to keep aleatory uncertainty at bay. At the
same time, though, project teams also develop mindful capabilities
to adapt to the epistemic uncertainties they face. These aspects of
rule- and Mindfulness-based resilience can appear contradictory and
can sometimes work in opposing directions. In this final section, we
will synthesise what has been written about project resilience and offer
a way forward while also appreciating how difficult it is to be resilient
in any true sense.

A ROAD MAP

T he previous chapters provided us with 'lures' that need to be
recognised, as they constrain our ability to manage uncertainty
effectively. These lead to a road map of Project Resilience, as shown in
Figure 8.1.

Our road map towards achieving these commonly accepted benefits
of project management may be slightly odd, different from what one
would expect. Your road map, of course, is likely to be very much
different from our suggested one. How would it look?

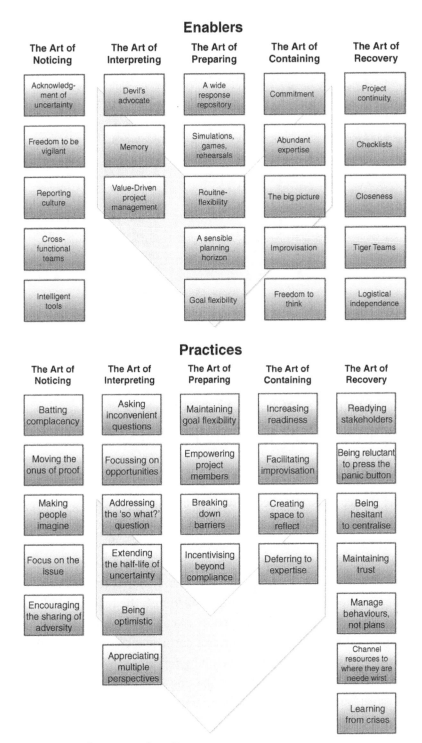

Enablers

The Art of Noticing	The Art of Interpreting	The Art of Preparing	The Art of Containing	The Art of Recovery
Acknowledgment of uncertainty	Devil's advocate	A wide response repository	Commitment	Project continuity
Freedom to be vigilant	Memory	Simulations, games, rehearsals	Abundant expertise	Checklists
Reporting culture	Value-Driven project management	Rouitne-flexibility	The big picture	Closeness
Cross-functional teams		A sensible planning horizon	Improvisation	Tiger Teams
Intelligent tools		Goal flexibility	Freedom to think	Logistical independence

Practices

The Art of Noticing	The Art of Interpreting	The Art of Preparing	The Art of Containing	The Art of Recovery
Batting complacency	Asking inconvenient questions	Maintaining goal flexibility	Increasing readiness	Readying stakeholders
Moving the onus of proof	Focussing on opportunities	Empowering project members	Facilitating improvisation	Being reluctant to press the panic button
Making people imagine	Addressing the 'so what?' question	Breaking down barriers	Creating space to reflect	Being hesitant to centralise
Focus on the issue	Extending the half-life of uncertainty	Incentivising beyond compliance	Deferring to expertise	Maintaining trust
Encouraging the sharing of adversity	Being optimistic			Manage behaviours, not plans
	Appreciating multiple perspectives			Channel resources to where they are neede wirst
				Learning from crises

Figure 8.1 *A road map towards resilience*

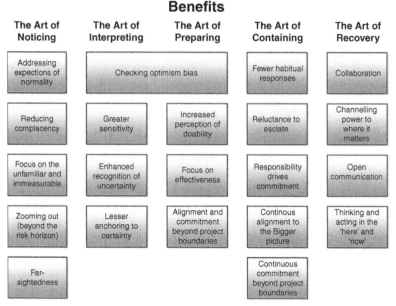

Benefits

The Art of Noticing	The Art of Interpreting	The Art of Preparing	The Art of Containing	The Art of Recovery
Addressing expections of normality	Checking optimism bias		Fewer habitual responses	Collaboration
Reducing complacency	Greater sensitivity	Increased perception of doability	Reluctance to esclate	Channelling power to where it matters
Focus on the unfamiliar and immeasurable	Enhanced recognition of uncertainty	Focus on effectiveness	Responsibility drives commitment	Open communication
Zooming out (beyond the risk horizon)	Lesser anchoring to certainty	Alignment and commitment beyond project boundaries	Continous alignment to the Bigger picture	Thinking and acting in the 'here' and 'now'
Far-sightedness			Continuous commitment beyond project boundaries	

Figure 8.1 *(Continued)*

BALANCING RULE-BASED AND MINDFULNESS-BASED PROJECT RESILIENCE

The strategy many projects adopt to manage uncertainty is to 'preload' categories and distinctions that have been identified from past experiences. This is often espoused as a 'self-evidently correct' deterministic and probabilistic approach and, indeed, on the face of it makes a lot of sense. Many of us may not even consider another method as this approach is so 'obvious'. The logic behind such an approach is clear – that resilience can be brought about by minimising the possibility of error as a consequence of fallible human cognition. This is achieved by developing repeatable, codified rules and procedures governing decision-making. The aim is to, as far as possible, 'automate' decisions from among a collection of past-informed choices.

Essentially, this orthodox approach to seek resilience is about making the *'best choice from among available options'*. We contend that the alternative is Mindfulness-based resilience, underpinned by the aim *'to create options'* (Langer 1997, 114). As outlined in the first two chapters of this book, Mindfulness in this context involves people being sensitive to and aware of their environment and conscious of the here-and-now rather than looking to the past (Langer 1989, 1997; Langer and Beard 2014). It is:

> *the combination of on-going scrutiny of existing expectations, continuous refinement and differentiation of expectations based on newer experiences, willingness and capability to invent new expectations that make sense of the unprecedented events, a more nuanced appreciation of context and ways to deal with it, and identification of new dimensions of context that improve foresight and current functioning.*
>
> (Weick and Sutcliffe 2007, 32)

What we are not saying is that there is no room at all for orthodox, compliance-focused uncertainty management. Instead, the aim is to develop project capabilities and behaviours that supplement traditional deterministic and probabilistic management approaches by encouraging situated human cognition, where more conventional approaches might not match the problem at hand. In other words, people working in projects are encouraged to complement standard responses with human expertise and judgement.

While we have advocated the role of mindful capabilities in facilitating positive project outcomes in uncertain environments, these need to be balanced with rule-based management. This could lead to potential tensions between the application of the two approaches. This raises an important question. If project practitioners are to act in a more mindful way when delivering their projects, how might this balance the need for both rule-based and Mindfulness-based management of uncertainty?

We identified five distinct ways of working which we were able to refine into models (or modes) of operation. We labelled these models respectively as *Rule-based, Entrepreneurial, Infusion, Just-in-time,* and *Recovery.*

Mode

Description of Mode

Rule-Based

The *Rule-based* mode is characterised by establishing preloaded responses pre-incident, to be activated post-incident. Once the incident is detected, we engage with the incident in a 'check-list' manner. In cases where we have to operate outside the 'rule book', because the prescribed response does not match the problem at hand, the power to make decisions migrates (is escalated) upwards to individuals with higher degrees of authority.

Entrepreneurial

The *Entrepreneurial* mode is to create and maintain permanent mindful capabilities. In comparison to the previous mode, there is limited pre-loading of responses; we are relatively 'free' to develop our own way of working. Compliance to a 'rule book' is replaced by project managers engaging with stakeholders in a discourse of what the problem constitutes and how best to solve it mindfully.

Infusion

Infusion is characterised by us dividing up our time to apply pre-loaded responses and the mindful creation of responses to manage the incident.

Just-in-time

The *Just-in-time* mode of reliable performance involves the creation of temporarily-deployed 'across-unit' capabilities to create a mindful response to an incident. This may take the form of a team of specialists in a particular field, 'Tiger Teams'.

Recovery

In cases of *Recovery*, a (radical) switch from rule- to mindfulness-based ways of working is driven typically by a crisis and the perception of intense pressure.

R=Rule-based; M=Mindfulness-based

Figure 8.2

RULE-BASED

The Rule-based approach is one of post-incident structural interdependence (across units) and temporal sequentiality (one after the other). It provides the advantage of efficient automation to an incident; pre-loaded responses are automatically activated once an incident is detected. The primary tension with this mode is one of switching from an automated response to one of Mindfulness if and when an automated response is not sufficient to tackle the incident as it develops. This often involves an escalation of the problem up the hierarchy of the project and the attendant issues that arise from such escalation, such as time lag and dodging of accountability. This is because we may lack the readiness, in terms of a repertoire of responses, to deal with problems that were not pre-planned, or to which existing frameworks do not provide an answer.

There may well be projects out there that are certain. In other words, one can predict and manage aleatoric uncertainty (risk), and foreknowledge is a sufficient basis for confidence in how the project will unfold. We can expect a minimal deviation from the plan; the goals are fixed and will not be challenged by internal or external influences. Stakeholders are predictable and amenable to the project objectives.

In this somewhat idealistic environment, the 'traditionally viewed' way of project management can – and should – be applied. The tools and techniques of the profession will serve well. The underlying premise is that pre-loaded plans and principles will sufficiently accommodate any form of adversity. Rule-based management as a pure form of planning and control is the dominant doctrine.

This approach to dealing with potential critical incidents offers a stable, transparent environment (because of pre-loading), in which external resources can be integrated relatively easily, as they only have to comply with a limited set of rules and procedures. The upside of a rule-based approach to managing projects by compliance is one of efficiency. Resources can be deployed as planned and can be (relatively) easily substituted. In some cases, this is a sensible approach, for example, where the work is comparatively routine and does not require much deep expertise; but in reality, this is uncommon.

Such preparedness is often, however, challenged by a lack of readiness to deal with problems that were not identified and pre-planned in advance of their occurrence. Particular challenges we observed were when issues arose where an employee (e.g. an engineer or project manager) could not solve the problem. This would result in the problem being escalated through the organisational hierarchy to managers with authority to decide how to tackle the problem. This could lead to delays and lengthy arguments about the root cause of incidents, especially in buyer-supplier relationships. This lack of a clear 'ownership' of the problem could result in both a lack of progress and a souring of relationships between parties involved, further exacerbating the situation. Most people can relate to such a situation, which can be attributed – to some extent – to the inadequacy of the applied doctrine of rule-based behaviour. We have observed, though, that this tends not to lead to a change in the way of working, so the scenario may be expected to repeat itself at a later point in time.

ENTREPRENEURIAL

In comparison to a Rule-based approach, the Entrepreneurial mode of resilience commences with a mindful setup of practices, which enables a constant creation of answers to problems in an environment where solutions were rarely evident in advance. Whereas an automated 'checklist'-like approach is predominant under the Rule-based approach, this mode emphasises a continuous process of critically evaluating alternative responses. In this context, there is no (or very limited) preloading of rules and procedures. We are 'free' to develop our own ways of working in contextually separated operations and projects.

This mode is appropriate for projects that are on 'high alert'. It generally involves providing an extensive – and sometimes idle – response repository for engaging with epistemic uncertainty. We have seen this used successfully in R&D projects and new product development groups where the environment is necessarily epistemically uncertain, the goals ambiguous and shifting and planning a project in detail at the outset is unlikely to reflect how the future will unfold. The problem with such an approach lies in establishing and maintaining a flexible culture of alertness, reporting and readiness to act on the unexpected. It is difficult to build a mindful project culture, yet relatively easy to undermine it by punishing unexpected failure, 'shooting the messenger' or sending the message that staff have transgressed protocols.

The potential difficulty with a fully mindful approach is that its value can erode over time if participants begin to believe that past actions will cover future problems. The purpose of Mindfulness, with all its ramifications, is to produce a state of constant challenge and questioning. This tends to be uncomfortable. It is important to be aware of the point at which we begin to believe that we have been successful in dealing with uncertainty – at this point, project managers need to reinforce the view that there will always be uncertainty out there that makes past action redundant.

INFUSION

The mode of Infusion is an attempt to combine both the worlds of Mindfulness and rule-based behaviour in a contextual, and continuous pre- and post-incident manner. The advantage is greater exploitation of past-applied solutions and the creation of future-applicable responses, providing greater efficiency but also readiness and preparedness to respond to the unknown. This mode involves invoking mindful capabilities, though not extra capacity, when pertinent.

In this scenario, we are generally compliant with rules and procedures, and in this sense, 'normal' operations can tend to look like those found in the Entrepreneurial mode mentioned previously. However, project managers are also explicitly empowered, authorised, and skilled to deal with situations that go beyond normality. Once an unexpected event strikes, they are prepared to deal with this situation and can 'switch' to a more mindful approach.

Although preparedness for dealing with uncertainty can be activated at any time, there are issues with this approach. The first one is overload. We may have our hands full dealing with the day-to-day activities of the project; therefore we may not have the extra capacity to be mindful and thus to be able to act in this way when required. Also, our readiness to enact these capabilities may be challenged by a reluctance to 'let go' of normality. This is a shift in emphasis that can be difficult. Similarly, we may be preoccupied with the new abnormality and, as a consequence, may focus on the urgent situation and largely ignore the rest of the project that still needs attention.

Mindful capabilities are often available pre-crisis and yet are exercised only minimally since the rule-based approach is dominant. Flexible responses under conditions of certainty are neither particularly warranted nor valuable, and the 'idleness' of this capability can be an issue. The Mindfulness response repertoire may begin to atrophy if not used, limiting our ability to call upon it in times of need. There is also a similar challenge with timely activation, as the leader may be reluctant to allow his or her additional mindful capacities to flourish. As we discussed previously, we may have inherent optimism that the current rule-based path is suitable for dealing with an event and, given our emotional attachment to the work, defer the deployment of mindful responses until it is perhaps too late. There is nothing malicious behind this; it is a simple acknowledgement of human nature that we tend to think that we are in control and that invoking special measures is unnecessary.

JUST-IN-TIME MINDFULNESS

In contrast to the Infusion approach, where we are required to produce resilience through dividing our time between adhering to a rulebook and creating responses mindfully, the Just-in-time mode involves providing additional staffing to develop the mindful capacities necessary to address the uncertain aspect of an incident. The idea is to automatically activate these other capacities and capabilities once an incident has been detected. This approach provides a more apparent distinction between the responsibilities of different staff with some dealing with the remaining business-as-usual and others, focusing on the unfolding uncertainty.

With the Just-in-time mode, the constraints of a Rule-based approach can be alleviated by the provision of additional mindful capacities. Most often, this happens via the *ad hoc* formation of Tiger Teams consisting of cross-functional experts. Such a team can be formed quickly to enable extra resources to be added at a time of need. This 'new' team, unencumbered by having worked on the project to date, can aid in the resolution of the critical incident in a mindful manner. This 'fresh set of eyes' can be beneficial, and can free up the existing project team to run normal operations and ensure that the parallel 'business as usual' aspects go smoothly.

The essential characteristic here is that mindful capabilities are deployed temporarily – to deal with specific events that have arisen – yet these are not the same resources as before. Additional capacity is 'parachuted-in' for a limited time until a state of normality has been re-established. Meanwhile, the already-deployed resources remain preoccupied with the day-to-day project activities. This is not necessarily straightforward, though. It requires the availability of the additional capacity, and they are unlikely to be on standby waiting to be called upon. Hence, the organisation's leaders must be ready to prioritise work rapidly and make decisions on resource deployment when necessary. This, itself, requires a flexible operating approach at the higher management levels.

RECOVERY

A final alternative for resilient performance, Recovery, stands out from the previously described approaches as this one is less deliberate but deployed as an extreme reaction to the situation. Under this mode, entire rule-based frameworks (such as risk registers) of past-informed responses are abandoned in the light of crisis-like incidents, to be replaced by mindful *ad hoc* practices for the crisis period. It is a mode that is often the result of failure to produce resilience through those modes that start off being predominantly rule-based (Rule-based, Infusion, Just-in-Time), often resulting in a crisis like-situation. Hence, it requires a radical temporal shift from rule-based to mindfulness-based management that may well be recognised as undesirable due to its disruptive transition from one mode to another.

ROCKS ON THE ROAD TO RESILIENCE

In this book we have suggested how one could – emphasis on could – overcome our innate human characteristics and manage a project in a mindful manner, as a means to address epistemic uncertainty. It is important to highlight some problems we are likely to face in trying to be resilient enough to weather any storm that might come along.

To reiterate, this book is not about a set of planning processes for the purpose of more significant prediction and control of aleatoric uncertainty. There are numerous standards that cover such frameworks and they do have their benefits. This is about project resilience in a wider sense, to allow people engaged in projects to be mindful; to activate situated human cognition to contain uncertainty. Project resilience is about:

1. making people uncomfortable about uncertainty in a mindful manner;
2. providing the comfort of resilience beyond the risk horizon.

First, we are constantly challenged by expectations of certainty and thus control. We vote for people who sell us an illusory world of stability, predictability, certainty and well-being. In turn, we expect others to plan and control the future, and project owners and sponsors also expect that of us. To put your hand up and argue that the world out there is largely unknowable is a daunting task. Anyone who has tried to 'sell' a project knows that it is more advantageous to pitch it as (reasonably) certain. Presenting your plan as largely unpredictable, but nonetheless resilient, is a tougher prospect. Even if both the presenter and the audience realise, deep-down, that there are aspects that remain unknowable, it is more comforting to go with a confident, 'traditional' planned approach. Of course, as long as this remains the case, life as a project manager is likely to be challenging and projects will continue to fail to meet their time and cost parameters and meet stakeholder expectations.

The certainty project sponsors crave is consistent with what we are longing for as individuals. We seek the comfort of certainty and the sense that we are in control of our project and us in it. By default, we try to build a comfort zone around ourselves. This book suggests that we, maybe tentatively at first, should step across this boundary, moving beyond the comfort of the risk horizon, and start creating a sense of unease about the unknown; that in turn triggers greater vigilance, preparedness, and readiness towards epistemic uncertainty.

TOOLKIT
SCENARIO PLANNING AND PREMORTEM

A plethora of literature exists about planning tools and techniques in project management. Much of such frameworks provide an authoritative account of what one should do. There appears to be less discourse about the assumptions underpinning these techniques, and therefore about the underlying basis for the planning techniques in use. One promising tool – scenario planning – stands out as driving mindful thinking, yet its use has not been widespread, and it is not often advocated within the project practitioner literature.

While scenario planning has its origins in military strategy studies, it was transformed into a business tool by, among others, Wack (e.g. Wack 1985) and Schoemaker (e.g. Schoemaker 1995). In contrast to risk management that drives the anticipation of individual risks, scenario planning caters for multiple future realities and encourages thinking in extremes, both possible and plausible.

The aim of scenario planning is the definition of a group of possible and plausible (not necessarily probable) futures that should constructively challenge each other. In comparison with traditional risk management, this approach does not aim to focus attention on quantifying a single future; instead, it provides multiple, more abstract projections of alternative futures.

Scenario planning is a powerful tool if applied in a non-threatening environment. For scenario planning to take effect, the culture of a project needs to be 'open-minded' with:

1. Receptiveness to multiple, sometimes divergent, perspectives.
2. Openness to having one's views questioned and challenged.
3. The use of a leader or facilitator who can manage the process of scenario planning in a controlled but non-threatening manner.
4. Willingness to provide resources to deal with essential issues that may occur.
5. Acknowledgement that scenarios are uncertain in their predictive power and that the 'truth' will not be forthcoming through this technique.

There is much written about scenario planning, so we will provide just a brief overview here of the critical stages to work through.

STEP 1: WHAT PROBLEM ARE YOU TRYING TO SOLVE?

This first step involves trying to understand the nature of the problem and thinking about potential solutions. The starting point involves devising a problem statement – a concise description of the problem. One way of outlining this is to produce a stakeholder map. This helps to make sense of the complexity involved in your project. We would recommend Peter Checkland's (1999) rich pictures that help to understand complex systems. Some of the questions to ask when developing these rich pictures and stakeholder maps are:

1. Who experiences the problem?
2. Who causes the problem?
3. Who pays for the problems?
4. Who supplies the solutions?
5. Who pays for the solutions?

The answers to these questions may help you to refine your problems, as well as inform your stakeholder analysis.

STEP 2: IDENTIFY TWO CRITICAL DIMENSIONS

First, come up with two dimensions that define your problem (in this case, uncertainty and uncontrollability). Next, plot your key drivers. Then, choose two drivers in the high uncertainty, high uncontrollability quadrant of the plot (in Figure 8.3, it is Driver B and C).

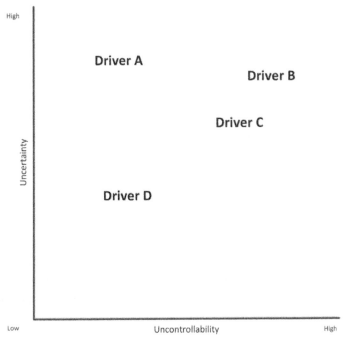

Figure 8.3 *Example of critical drivers*

STEP 3: CREATE SCENARIOS

You have identified two highly uncontrollable, highly uncertain drivers. Next, you must envision the extreme conditions for each driver: extreme positive versus extreme negative, extremely optimistic versus extremely pessimistic. Now, draw another four-quadrant plot, with the extremes of critical uncertainties on the axes.

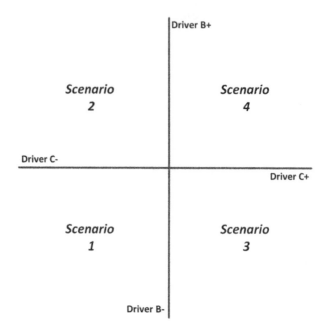

Figure 8.4 *Example of scenario creation in reference to two critical uncertainties (B and C)*

STEP 4: COMPOSE THE STORIES

For each of your four scenarios, you must now write a short story. It has been found that organisational stories are very effective at capturing the imagination and giving issues far more immediacy (Denning 2004). Each story should 'capture' a vision of future states of a project. It can be quite beneficial to come up with a catchy name for each scenario; names stick in mind and capture the essence.

STEP 5: SCENARIO APPLICATION

Given your four short stories, it is time to return to the original question. When you first asked the question, you could not come up with a conclusive answer, because you did not know what the future looks like. But now you have four visions of the future!

STEP 6: FOCUS YOUR ATTENTION ON YOUR WORST-CASE SCENARIO (-/- SCENARIO)

Introduce your team to the exercise by informing everyone that the project has failed spectacularly in line with your defined worst-case scenario. Clearly explain the consequences of your worst-case scenario in terms of stakeholder dissatisfaction and implications for project deliverables, for example.

STEP 7: EVALUATION OF CRITICAL UNCERTAINTIES (PREMORTEM)

Please evaluate in line with your defined critical uncertainties (see Figure 8.2) whether and how you can prevent your worst-case scenario from materialising. If, for example, you have classified most of your critical uncertainties as uncertain and uncontrollable, the likelihood of averting a worst-case scenario is very low.

STEP 8: REVIEW AND PRIORITISE ACTIONS

Prioritise and develop managerial interventions that are controllable and for which you can define a certain impact. In line with your critical uncertainties, determine a key intervention, and possibly visualise this intervention on the very same Figure 8.4 analysis.

What is mindful about scenario planning and a premortem?
Scenario planning exercises such as the one described before, for example, open decision-makers to numerous, plausible alternative 'stories of the future' that inherently challenge assumptions and mindsets. Corporations including Shell and governments

including Singapore have used such practices – first and foremost for their heuristic value – with considerable success for decades. Much like being mindful, the practice of nonjudgmentally assessing different plausible futures is a practical way of shining light on old unexamined thought patterns and making room for new ideas.

Traditional project management techniques enable us to plan for a single future in a deterministic, probabilistic fashion. Hence, reinforcing this 'anchor', driven into the 'ground' – our expectations – and allowing it to drive our actions in a preloaded, autopilot manner. Scenario planning though enables us to 'zoom out' beyond that single prediction of a plan. Our mind is challenged by the definition of multiple and extreme scenarios.

A project premortem is a strategy for assessing the strength of a project before it ever happens. For project leaders and team members, the premortem works by assuming the worst – that the project has failed – and then looking for all the ways and reasons why. By doing this, the team can figure out where potential problems lie and what pitfalls may present themselves to avoid disaster and help the project succeed.

In essence, a premortem focusses our mind to how we can prevent a worst-case scenario from happening. As such, we may change our way of engaging with a project: Instead of 'selling' the illusion of certainty, we draw our and our stakeholder's attention towards our capability to prevent a worst-case scenario from materialising, with the option of ending up with more beneficial alternative scenarios.

In essence, scenario planning makes us more uncomfortable, as a trigger of mindful thinking, generating a more discriminatory view beyond the risk horizon. Nevertheless, it also focuses our attention to those capabilities that are required to avert a crisis in the first place.

Let us now consider resilience along the lines of S.M.A.R.T. goal-setting:

- Specific. Resilience remains mainly unspecific, as it relates to human behaviour under a range of different conditions. It cannot be clearly defined or identified according to a given set of practices one has to carry out. In fact, since it is context-specific it thus requires – every time from scratch – a unique match between a problem and a solution. The details of each case will vary. The containment can be prepared and readied for, yet the responses need to be crafted according to unfolding events.
- Measurable. The costs of resilience may be immediately measurable whereas the benefits may be far less tangible. The expected effect of being mindfully resilient is based to some extent on faith rather than unarguable financial measurement. The value of resilience could be quantified by the absence of failure. Nevertheless, if such an assessment can only be carried out ex-post, then what benefit does it have?
- Attainable. Unfortunately, there is no agreed state of resilience that is 'good enough' for a project. A state of resilience is an ideal one that that the project team can aspire to, but it is a continual journey rather than a destination. One may consider developing levels of 'resilience maturity', yet it is difficult to take into account the ever-changing nature of risk, uncertainty and complexity.
- Relevant. This aspect is in the eye of the beholder and depends on the context. Resilience will probably focus on mindful practices, rather than having choices overly constrained by the rigid application of rules and procedures. Relevance needs to be considered with regard to the localised assessment of risk, uncertainty, and complexity.
- Time-based. Project Management is a permanent state of rule- and Mindfulness-based resilience. The only time-based dimension refers to when the project context changes and the team needs to adapt to a shifting environment.

Does this imply that mindful Project Management is an elusive concept, as it is not S.M.A.R.T.? Yes and No. The 'patchwork' of lures, best practices and suggestions may be turned into a step-by-step guide to follow and apply. S.M.A.R.T. but not 'smart', as the underlying context is central to the choices that need to be made. We would advise against turning the insights of this book into an 'autopilot'. Acknowledge and embrace the lack of specificity, measurability, and attainability and use these voids to think about what you can do afresh on your latest project. Try and resist the temptation to think that only what is measurable is automatically good. Resilience is a state, seemingly elusive, often apparently just out of reach. We strive for it, challenge it constantly, yet never manage to reach that ideal state that makes a project truly failsafe. Do you feel uncomfortable enough with this truth?

MINDFUL PRACTICES
OUR CASE COMPANIES

In order to develop these small vignettes of mindful practices, TTP, Aviva, and Intel allowed us to have some insights into their management of projects. In this respect, we are very grateful to have spent time with some of their project managers. Richard Mason and Simon Kelly of Intel talked us through some of the projects they have been involved in. Lynn Newman from Aviva elaborated on best practices, and Tristan Barkley and Piers Harding from TTP provided us with plenty of information about their radical innovation projects.

We asked somewhat naive questions about how to manage uncertainty. The purpose was to unravel the obvious. The case companies said that they 'just do' this because they believe it is the right thing to do, although at times they are not aware 'why'.

Despite the number of vignettes, neither we nor the respondents claim that these projects are perfectly managed, in a mindful manner; these projects are not 'fail-safe'. Yet, we have chosen these organisations as we believe they each go beyond process, do not put being compliant to rules and procedures centre-stage, and exploit the power of the human mind to deal in particular with uncertainty.

Being resilient through reliance on rule-based and Mindfulness-based management is the pursuit of an ideal state, which we can never fully achieve. We can only strive for it; and so do these organisations.

OUTLOOK

The concept of resilience through aspects of Mindfulness, in projects, is not new to either academics or practitioners. There is, though, a plethora of evidence about the usefulness of reducing human cognition as a source of error by replacing it with rules, applied consistently and transparently. The weight of such evidence seems overwhelming, measured by the number of planning processes and associated accreditation programmes being advocated as 'self evidently correct'.

Nevertheless, there is growing concern about this single-minded approach to managing uncertainty in a past-informed, rule-based manner. This is underlined by significant disasters resulting in injury, loss of life and substantial financial costs. Some alternative approaches are being considered, focusing on the contribution of the mind. However, these progressive discussions on how situated human cognition can benefit the management of uncertainty do not appear to be part of the mainstream of project management, at least from a practitioner's perspective. There is still a very much unchallenged pursuit of ever greater consistency of action. Although our book should be understood as a challenge to conventional wisdom in project management, we cannot claim that it provides the 'Holy Grail' for managing uncertainty. Evidence about Mindfulness and its impact is still limited, although growing, and so this book is more a proposition than a prescription. Its purpose is fulfilled even if you disagree with everything we said. A disagreement is a form of reflection, and this book should be a basis for reflection.

You might think after having read all about lures, biases, and practices that you already experience all these and that this reflects your reality. It might all be evident to you and only highlight aspects that you already know. If this is the case, is your project approach as good as it gets? The concept of the resilient project does not claim to offer a universal, complete, set of practices. You probably do much more than has been covered in this book. Bear that in mind, and ask yourself 'why' you do what you do. Does it help you to:

- **Notice** beyond the risk horizon?
- **Interpret** epistemic uncertainty with greater scrutiny?
- **Prepare** yourself better for the effects of epistemic uncertainty?
- **Contain** epistemic uncertainty in a more timely and appropriate manner, to prevent a crisis in the first place?
- **Recover** faster and more effectively from a crisis?

This book may have helped to start important conversations and may have raised pertinent questions. We hope that our suggestions have been valuable. Our wish is to turn the idea of resilience through Mindfulness from an abstract notion to a set of behaviours that make it real for you in your projects.

REFERENCES

Checkland, P. 1999. *Systems Thinking, Systems Practice*. Chichester: Wiley.

Denning, S. 2004. "Telling Tales." *Harvard Business Review* 82(5): 122–29.

Langer, E. J. 1989. *Mindfulness*. Cambridge: Perseus Publishing.

Langer, E. J. 1997. *The Power of Mindful Learning. Reading*, MA: Addison-Wesley.

Langer, E. J., and A. Beard. 2014. "Mindfulness in the Age of Complexity." *Harvard Business Review* no. March issue: 68–73.

Schoemaker, P. 1995. "Scenario Planning: A Tool for Strategic Thinking." *Sloan Management Review* 36(2): 25–40.

Wack, P. 1985. "Scenarios: Unchartered Waters Ahead." *Harvard Business Review* 63(5): 73–89.

Weick, K., and K. Sutcliffe. 2007. *Managing the Unexpected: Resilient Performance in an Age of Uncertainty*. 2nd. San Francisco: Jossey Bass.

INDEX

Page numbers in **bold** refer to content in **figures**; page numbers in *italics* refer to content in *tables*.

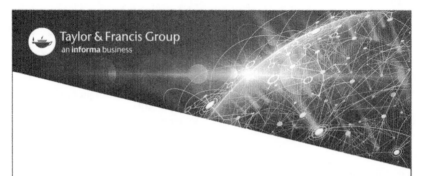